INCOME STREAMS

ARVIND UPADHYAY

This is a book about making money on the Internet. Rather than spouting obsolete statistics about how many gazillions of people are getting online every minute, about how many trillions of dollars' worth of stuff is being sold on the Internet, or about how the Internet is changing the world—yadda, yadda, yadda—let's just cut to the chase. Let me show you the money . . . or more precisely, the e-money. In this chapter, I describe how, using the principles in this book, I earned almost $100,000 cash in only 24 hours using the Internet. Then I will show you how you can do exactly what I have done. Does that get your heart racing? In my previous three New York Times best-sellers, Nothing Down, Creating Wealth, and Multiple Streams of Income, I've helped thousands of people to achieve financial freedom—even to become millionaires and multimillionaires. Now it's your turn.

Your Next Fortune Is Only a Click Away Although I've been in business for over 20 years, I was slow to adopt the power of the Internet to market my own seminars and information products. I wasn't alone. Even today, tens of millions of businesses, small and large, still haven't tapped into this power. For me, it took something dramatic to open my eyes. In the fall of 1998, a friend, David LeDoux, called excitedly to tell me how he had stumbled onto an interesting method of marketing using the Internet. "Bob," he said, "I made $13,000 in one day!" I was intrigued. "How did you do it?" "Rather than tell you, let me show you." A few days later, sitting at the keyboard of my home office computer in San Diego, California, David explained how he was attracting visitors to his recently launched Web site. Many of these visitors registered for his free Internet newsletter. After only a few short months, he managed to accumulate about 1,500 subscribers. Every week he sent an e-mail to his growing list of subscribers sharing his latest research. In each e-newsletter (called an e-zine}, he included advertisements for other products or services. He explained that because the e-mails cost him almost nothing to send, the sales he made were extremely profitable: "Let me show you how it works. Right now, before your very eyes, I'm going to make some money for you." Yes, he had my attention. Using my computer, he composed a short e-mail message. It read something like this: Hello, again. This is David. At this very moment I am sitting in the home office of best-selling author Robert

G. Allen. Through his # I best-selling books and audio programs, he has helped thousands of people become millionaires. His hottest-selling audio program, Multiple Streams of Income, is marketed for $60 through Nightingale/Conant. I've prevailed upon Mr. Allen to offer you this popular program at a reduced price. For the next 60 minutes only, he has agreed to let any of my subscribers purchase his powerful sixtape program for only $29.95. If you're interested, please respond immediately with your name, address, and credit card number with expiration date. Have a nice day. David. He asked me to verify the exact time. Then he sent the message to his 1,500 subscribers. I had no idea what to expect. Sixty-one seconds later, the first response arrived. Ding! (Does your e-mail make a sound when you receive a message?) This first response included a full address and complete credit card information. Over the next hour, as David was trying to explain to me the benefits of marketing over the Internet, I could hardly pay attention. I just kept listening to the sound of each e-mail response—Ka-ching! Ka-ching! Ka-ching! Hundreds of dollars of orders. I was amazed. In front of my eyes, with very little marketing cost and almost no effort, he had generated a tidy profit for me. But it wasn't the instant profit that excited me. It was the potential for huge streams of cash flow with almost zero marketing costs. Do the math with me. Suppose you want to market a $100 audio program in the bricks-andmortar world. You rent a mailing list of 10,000 target prospects, create a direct mail letter, and pay for postage. All told, it will cost in excess of 50 cents per letter just to drop the letters in the mail. In other words, it will cost a minimum of $5,000 to mail 10,000 marketing pieces. However, the response rate through direct mail is usually less than onehalf of 1 percent, which means that these 10,000 letters may generate only 50 paid responses. Fifty customers at $100 apiece is $5,000—just enough to recoup your mailing costs. There's no money left to pay for the tapes, the packaging, and the postage to send the product to the customer via snail mail. You've lost money! Now, let's assume we do the same mailing using the Internet. This time, however, instead of marketing an audiocassette program, we offer a package of powerful information—digital special reports, digital books, even digital video and audio in a powerful multimedia presentation. Since the information is digital, it can be delivered over the Internet instantly at almost zero cost. Now let's send

10,000 e-mails to a list of targeted e-mail prospects assuming the same one-half of 1 percent response rate. We generate the same 50 orders at $100 apiece, except this time the marketing costs and the product costs are nearly zero. The entire $5,000 in proceeds is almost pure profit! Did you get that? Let's do a profit and loss statement for our new Internet business:Marketing costs 0 Product costs 0 Shipping charges 0 Credit card charges 5% Profit 97% Now, let's think big. If 10,000 e-mails generate $5,000, then 100,000 e-mails produce $50,000, right? And a million e-mails could generate a $500,000 profit! Talk about a bottom line! What if you did this once a month? Heck, once a week?! Now you can see why I was so excited. I began immediately to develop my own Web site. After several false starts, we finally launched during the first week of August 2019. Using various methods (which I'm going to teach you), during the next nine months we gathered an opt-in list of over 11,500 subscribers to my free Internet newsletter. (Just to set the record straight, I don't believe in sending unauthorized e-mail, or spam, and nothing I teach you will resemble anything illegal, immoral, or in violation of the spirit of the Internet.) People often say that those who ask for free information are not willing to spend money. They're just "looky-loos." This is generally correct. The vast majority of the "free" subscribers to my Web site are not willing to spend a penny on any of my products or services. They are perfectly content to sample my free offerings. However, I also know that if the offer is right, a small percentage of any interested audience (free or paying) can be enticed to open up their wallets or purses. Let's put this theory to the test. . . for real."Sit me at the keyboard of any computer in the world with access to the Internet, and In just 24 hours I'll earn at least $24,000 in cash." The producers of the show were skeptical. They wanted me to lower the figure. They reasoned, "A thousand dollars in 24 hours is still a lot of money to the average person." I must admit that I, too, had my doubts, but I just had a gut feeling that, given 24 hours, I could generate at least $24,000. Maybe more. On May 24, 2000, at a studio in Burbank, California, at exactly 12:38 P.M., in front of live cameras, I sat down at the keyboard of a computer belonging to the producer of the shoot, Packy McFarland. With a simple click of the mouse, I sent a special message to my list of 11,518 subscribers. Would anyone respond with cash? Frankly, I had no idea. This was marketing without a safety net. The first order was generated in less than four minutes. A man in Houston sent me $2,991. The second order came from my friend, David LeDoux. He had been monitoring my progress and sent me $200. Thereafter, every several minutes another order ka-chinged into my email box. After 6 hours and 11 minutes the total was . . . $46,684.95! I slept very peacefully that night. I was convinced that while I slept even more orders would pour in. I was right. The next morning, still dressed in my bathrobe, with live cameras rolling, I checked the total number of orders. It was now up to . . . $78,827.44! This was exciting! And I still had about four hours to go. That afternoon, 24 hours after the challenge had begun, we did a final tally. The total was . . . $94,532.44Almost $100,000 in just one day! And the orders kept pouring in. Within just a few days the total had climbed to over $115,000. Before you get too excited, let me remind you that it had actually taken over nine months to set up this process. I had to launch the Web site. I had to draw traffic to my site. I had to gather the names of people for my Internet newsletter. But what if you could work for a full year with zero income and then, in one day, recoup all of your expenses and walk away with a net profit of $10,000 . . . $30,000 . . . $50,000 . . . maybe even $100,000? Moreover, what if you could repeat this process once a month for the rest of your life?! Would that be worth the effort? This book takes you step by step through the process that I used to achieve such incredible results. Although the product I was marketing was an information product, these same principles can be used to market anything—products, services, even business opportunities.

Now, that you know the results of my live Internet challenge, I'd like to take you behind the scenes and teach you the timeless marketing principles I used to increase the odds of success. The serious planning began about 60 days before the May 24 shooting date. My first step was to call on my mentors. I can't stress enough the importance of building a powerful mastermind team. Successful people rely heavily on their mentors. Ordinary people don't. It's that simple. My marketing team consisted of Tom Painter, Daren Falter, Bob Gatchel, Saul Klein, Mike Barnett, Ken Kerr, Ken Varga, and Scott Haines, supplemented by conversations with at least a dozen others. Here's how I presented the concept to my mentors: "Suppose you have a goal to market a product and earn $24,000 in 24 hours using the Internet. Suppose it's more than a goal—suppose your life is on the line. If you succeed, you get to live. If you fail, you face the firing squad. How would you do it?" In other words, what if your life literally depended upon your success? Would you prepare differently? Most people try things. I don't. As Yoda taught Luke Skywalker, there is no try. There is either do or do not. When I design a marketing campaign, I assume that it must work. I plan for zero failure. It either works or I die. Of course, I don't really expect to die . . . but I put that kind of intensity into the design. I don't expect to fail. I expect to win. When Spanish explorer Hernan Cortes conquered Mexico in 1519, he faced overwhelming odds . . . tens of thousands of Aztec warriors against his 400 soldiers. When his troops began to mutiny, Cortes ordered all but one of his 11 ships to be scuttled and sunk so there was no avenue of escape. Then he rallied his troops with a stirring speech. Conquer or die. Those were the options. When I gave this do-or-die scenario to my mentors, it focused their advice to me. They thought about it in a different way. Instead of bouncing around a few nice ideas, I got their best advice: "Well, Bob, if my life were on the line, then here is what I would do." In the next chapter, I share what they told me. Obviously, it worked.

Contents

Foreword

Imagine making money while you sleep. Imagine waking up richer every morning than when you went to bed the night before. Imagine receiving streams of money from people all over the world. Imagine a business that operates on automatic pilot— whether you show up or not. Imagine low overhead and high profits. Imagine operating your business from exotic worldwide locations—from a cell phone on the beach in Tahiti or from your laptop in a restaurant atop the Eiffel Tower. If you can imagine these things, you can achieve them using the vehicle of the Internet. I'm so excited to be sharing this information with you. I know that if you follow the strategies and techniques in this book, you will be well on your way to Internet riches and a lifestyle that will be envied by almost everyone you meet.If you ask most fledgling entrepreneurs why they want to be in business the usual answer is "to make some money." But when you pin them down with some more probing questions, it will most likely boil down to something like this. . . . After I've taken care of my basic needs, I want to be free . . . To do what I want When I want Where I want With whomever I want For as long as I want Without having to worry about money. Does that describe you? If so, then let's make sure that the by-product of your start-up Internet business is freedom. It's not to sell a bunch of stuff, or to get 15 gazillion hits a day, or to hire 1,000 employees, or have the coolest graphics, or to have the fastest-growing company in the world, or to have the best products, or to get your name in the paper, or to launch an IPO. Some of these things may even be counterproductive to obtaining freedom. If freedom is your goal, don't lose sight of it. I mention this because thousands of beginning entrepreneurs launch new businesses each week without asking this all-important question: Why are we doing this? If they do ask, they usually come up with the following answer: "Because we want to break free from our jobs." Therefore, they escape the low-paying "job prison" for a potentially higher-paying "self-employment prison." Even if you trade golden handcuffs for platinum handcuffs, you're still locked up Your Internet Business. A Freedom Machine With that in mind, let's design a way to make the most money in the least time that will lead to the greatest freedom. Agreed? In this book I show multiple ways for the average nontechie to earn serious amounts of income from the Internet. This is 24/ 7/365 money . . . the kind of income that most people only dream about.

And it can happen fast.

Preface

Timeless Principles of Marketing Applied to Explosive Growth of the Internet The success of any business venture boils down to using timeless principles of marketing. According to marketing guru Jay Abraham, a marketer has only three basic goals: 1. To increase the number of customers 2. To increase the amount of the average order 3. To increase the frequency of orders That's it. There ain't no more. If you can master these three fundamentals, you can grow any business, whether you're on the Internet or not. It doesn't matter whether your product is information or a fly swatter. If you understand marketing, you can make serious income. If you don't understand marketing, your business is going to die. I understand marketing. In the past 20 years, through trial and error, I have marketed over $250 million worth of information with my name on it. For the first time, I offer in print what I've learned about marketing in my career. I believe that anyone can learn these timeless principles and double their current business in less than a year . . . even without utilizing the Internet. Any current or future entrepreneur will profit from reading this book. But those who wish to profit from the Internet must learn these timeless principles of marketing or they will end up in the dot-corn graveyard The world of technology is changing so rapidly that a book like this can be outdated before the manuscript makes it to press. Because this book is based on timeless principles of marketing, I want you to be able to pick it up 10 years from now and still find relevant strategies for creating endless cash flow. Finally, I've aimed to make this more than a book about business on the Internet. This is a business in a book. This is not just a book that you read. It is a book that you do. We don't just talk about making money. When you are finished with the last chapter, I want you to be online and actually earning steady streams of cash—starting from scratch. Is this possible? Well, I'm famous for my challenges. When I wrote my first book, Nothing Down, I threw down the following gauntlet: "Send me to any city. Take away my wallet. Give me $100 for living expenses. And in 72 hours I'll buy an excellent piece of real estate using none of my own money."

CHAPTER ONE

How to Guarantee Your Success on the Internet

There is a growing digital divide in the world—a chasm between the digital haves and the digital have-nots. Despite the excitement about the advantages of marketing on the Internet, millions of Web site owners have been and will continue to be baffled by the Internet and disappointed with the results of their online experience. There seem to be so many new terms to learn—autoresponders, list serves, affiliate programs, viral marketing, and stickiness. If you're a veteran of the Internet, these terms are familiar to you. But if you're a beginner, the process can be intimidating. There is a phrase that I learned early in my career. "A confused mind always says no." In this rapidly changing world, with new technological marvels being introduced daily, it's almost impossible not to be confused and overwhelmed. Precisely because things are moving so quickly, you don't have time to be confused—you must decide to say yes to marketing on the Internet. You do not want to be left behind. There's just too much money at stake. In my opinion, however, the reason people don't make money on the Net is not because of technophobia. It is because people are confused about the concepts of basic marketing. Look at the millions of dollars

that have been burned on ineffective Internet marketing campaigns. It's a crime. Really. People ought to be locked up for squandering so much good money. I personally made more "Net" profit in one day than Amazon.com made in its first five years. Of course, I'm not a billionaire, either. But I don't count my worth in stock certificates. I count my worth the way ordinary people do—by how much spendable cash flow it generates now. Ultimately, this is the way Wall Street also evaluates companies. If a company continues to lose money, it eventually becomes toast. I'm just more impatient than Wall Street. I like to make profit from day one. And so should you. So, what is the most fundamental principle of all marketing? Gary Halbert, the marketing guru, poses a famous riddle: Suppose you're given the opportunity to launch a hot dog stand on the beach right next to a competing hot dog stand. If you could choose one marketing advantage over your competitor, what would you choose? Would it be a more favorable location, higher-quality ingredients, the world's best advertising copy, or the most beautiful waitresses? Gary says he would only want one advantage: a starving crowd! Too often, people launch new products and then go searching for a market. You must reverse the process: Find a hungry market in search of a product. The most important marketing question is, "How can I identify a hungry group of people and then create a feeding frenzy?" If you can answer this question, you will be miles ahead of those cashpoor, equity-rich Internet start-ups. You will sail across the digital divide on the wings of cash flow while your foolish competitors crash and burn.

Three Important Questions

My mentors reminded me that any marketing campaign—especially on the Net—must answer three questions:

1. Who is your target audience? 2. What do they want? 3. How can you motivate this target audience to act now? Most beginning marketers spend 90 percent of their time creating the perfect product and 10 percent of their time finding a perfect audience. The secret is to reverse the ratio: Spend 90 percent of your time finding the right audience. I call this finding hungry fish. I prefer to find a school of fish in a feeding frenzy. If you drop your bait (advertising) into such a school of hungry fish, they will attack that bait (ad)—even if it's written by an amateur. Where do you find the schools of customers like this? You have two choices: (1) You can either drop your bait into someone else's lake or (2) create your own lake and spawn your own fish. If you are fishing in other people's lakes, you have to pay them for the privilege. In other words, you have to pay to advertise in their magazines, newsletters, or on their radio or TV stations. Or you'll have to pay a fee to rent names from their private mailing lists. This is the fastest way to find a group of hungry fish . . . but it is also the most expensive.A slower method is to create your own lake and spawn your own fish. In this case, you also have control over your marketing project and at a much lower long-term cost.

In planning to make $24,000 in 24 hours I could have chosen the fast, simple, easy route by renting or buying one of the many e-mail lists available on the Internet. (In Chapter 6 I will show you how to profitably access such lists.) The disadvantage to this method is that it costs money . . . and if you're like the average entrepreneur, money can be scarce. I decided instead to take the slower route and build my own *list. The wiser choice for you will be to test your ideas with inexpensive rented lists and, once your business concept is viable, to build your business with a combination of targeted paid advertising while simultaneously spawning your own list of interested customers. When I launched my own Web site, one of its major features was a free e-zine called the Streams of Cash E-Letter. I encouraged all visitors to my site to leave their e-mail addresses. Using various methods, over the next several months, the subscriber list to my infrequent newsletter grew. Nine months later, the list had over 11,000 subscribers. These people opted in to an e-mail list . . . they are willing recipients. In other words, when I send an e-mail message to anyone on this list, it is not spam (unwanted or unsolicited e-mail). In later chapters, I'll show you how to use this technique and many others. Although it took many months to build my list, I felt it was the best solution to creating a lifetime cash flow. This is the list I used for my Internet challenge. I had used the list for research, but I had never marketed a single product to the people on the list. The question remained: Would this list of freebie subscribers be willing to open up their wallets or purses and actually buy anything? Would I be willing to bet my life on it? When I agreed to the Internet challenge, there was a lot of doubt about whether this was a realistic goal. One thing I had going for me was my knowledge of marketing. Marketing is the science of encouraging interested people to buy. If you make a powerful offer in the right way to an interested audience, you should be able to motivate that audience to buy. Exactly 14 days before May 24, I began a series of five messages to those on my e-mail list to prepare them for my Internet challenge. Imagine checking your e-mail and receiving a message with the following summary in the Subject line. Would you open it? From Subject Robert Allen Making massive amounts of money on the Net As you read the following message, remember that it was being sent to a group of prequalified readers. Therefore, the message is longer than traditional marketing missives. Read it for yourself and try to detect which principles of marketing I am using to create massive action by my dropdead date of May 24.*

17 Message # I May 10,2000 To: Subscribers to Arvind 's Streams of Cash E-Letter From: # I Best-selling financial author, Arvind Upadhyay Re: Making massive amounts of money on the net Message I of 5 You could win thousands of dollars in CASH as a result of reading this e-mail. As a subscriber to my free Streams of Cash E-Letter, you will be receiving a series of five extremely important messages from me over the next 14 days. On May 24, the final of the five messages will be sent to you at about noon Pacific standard time. As a reward for reading this fifth and final message, I will randomly select several subscribers to receive CASH awards of $ 1,000, $500, $250, $ 100, and $50, respectively, and at least 100 Of you will receive free autographed copies of one of my best-selling books, The Road to Wealth.

Why am I doing this? I think you'll be very interested in my reason.... But first—some news hot off the presses: My brand-new book, Multiple Streams of Income, just hit # 12 on the Wall Street Journal business best-seller list as of Friday, April 29. People are raving that it's my best book ever. Check out the rave reviews by clicking on the link to Amazon.com at the end of this message. I want to thank those of you who helped me select the subtitle—IIow to Generate a Lifetime of Unlimited Wealth. It's obviously working. I got word today that Staples just ordered 3,000 copies. If you've already bought the book, make sure you take advantage of the FREE four-week live teleconference with *me personally (valued at $250). The number to register for this FREE teleclass is on page vii of the Multiple Streams of Income book. Now for the meat of this e-letter: How to Moke $24,000 Cash in 24 Hours on the Internet. I am shooting a new TV infomercial with Guthy/Renker, the folks who produced Tony Robbins's megasuccessful show. Last weekend, the producers flew many of my millionaire success stories to Los Angeles to film their amazing testimonials. I am constantly astonished by how much money my students are making—literally millions. (Who needs Regis?) As a part of this show, I'm going to do a live INSTANT CASH challenge. On television, with live cameras rolling, I am going to demonstrate how to make INSTANT CASH from the Internet. On May 24, at about noon Pacific standard time, we will film the segment where, with just one click of my mouse, I will activate an avalanche of cash flowing into my e-mail box. The goal is to make a minimum of $24,000 in 24 hours. Here's the $24,000 question: Is it possible for YOU to make more money in a day than the average person corns in an entire year? Would you like to learn how to do this? If you're interested in learning how to do this, watch your e-mail over the next 14 days. I will guide you through the process IN ADVANCE. You will be the very first group of people on planet Earth to learn how I plan on doing this. And DON'T MISS THE FINAL MESSAGE on May 24. Even if you're away from your computer, check your e-mail on that day.*

That was the first message. Let's examine it to learn why it was an effective marketing message. First of all, the subject is about making massive amounts of money on the Net. If this doesn't interest you, better check your pulse—you might be dead. This is the bait that hooks readers into continuing to read further. There are several other persuasive hooks throughout this message, but at the risk of belaboring the point, I want to remind you that "making massive amounts of money on the Net" would not have been an effective message if addressed to the wrong audience. Remember, this was my lake, and this message was just the kind of bait my fish were hungry for. For your message to be effective, it must hit the hot button of your tar-get audience. Do you know what their hot buttons are? Don't just guess what they want—or give them what you want hoping that they also want it. Ask them what they want!! That is exactly what I did in the very next e-mail message. The second message in the series was sent five days after the first. Once again, it is a very long e-mail—which breaks all the rules of traditional e-mail marketing—but something hidden in this e-mail message causes a very large number of people to read every single word! As you read it, see if you can spot any of the principles that make this message effective. Imagine getting the following message in your e-mail box. Would you open it?

It must have taken some people upwards of half an hour to complete it. Still, I asked my subscribers to help me decide what I should offer. In other words, I asked them to vote for what they would like to buy. Of course, their feedback is risk-free. They don't have to buy anything. I even offer to send them a special report as my thanks for their input. They are simply asked to tell me what they might like if the price were right. Then I ask them to name their price. The power of this strategy is that it offers people a riskless action. Enticing your customers to take baby steps is extremely important. In a later chapter I'll share with you why it's so important, but first I want you to see the results. Guess how many people responded to my survey? I received almost 2,000 responses in less than 24 hours! That's close to a 20 percent response. I was completely astounded. Table 2.2 shows the results tabulated by my partner and marketing guru, Tom Painter. See if you can learn anything from these results.

Having this information was extremely important in designing the ultimate offer. It let me know that a higher price was possible over the Internet. Gathering this data also let me know which offers I should not include in the final list and which offers I could bundle together. Now, let's review. The most important marketing advice you can ever receive is as follows: Find the right audience. Ask people what they want. Give it to them.

CHAPTER TWO

A Few Simple Strategies Can Make You Rich

I'm a big believer in "simple and easy." Beats "complicated and hard" every time. Rather than bludgeon you with an encyclopedia of marketing, including 1,001 ways to write super headlines, 196 ways to generate new leads, and 67 ways to get people to say yes, let's start with the fundamentals. Besides, according to the 80/20 principle, 20 percent of your marketing ideas will produce 80 percent of your results. So let's boil marketing down to a few bedrock principles. Do these few things well and you'll likely be successful. Don't do these critical few things and all the other ideas combined still won't save you. According to marketing guru Jay Abraham, when you boil business down to its basics, a businessperson is trying to master only three major activities: 1. To increase the number of customers 2. To persuade these customers to buy more in their initial orders 3. To encourage these customers to buy more frequently More customers. Larger orders. More often. Got it? If you're starting a new business, these are the three buttons you push to get your business off the ground. If your existing business is in trouble, these are the three buttons you push to make it healthy again. Getting more customers

is all about generating leads—getting your .message in front of the right people and enticing them to take a look at your business. Increasing the average order is about persuasion and bundling—giving people a better deal for a larger order. Increasing the frequency of purchase is about the back end—developing long-term relationships with your customers so they want to buy again and again. In this book, I'll teach you how to accomplish all three of these major activities. And I'll translate these concepts into simple language because I'm always amazed by how people try to complicate things. Here's a great story to illustrate my point. Charles Jarvis, the great American humorist, tells the story about the man who goes into the pet store to buy a pet bird. He sees dozens of caged birds with tiny price tags dangling from their little legs. He scans each price tag one by one: $5, $5, $5 . . . $50! "Hmmm," he wonders. "This $50 bird looks like all of the others. What could be special about this one?" He asks the store clerk. The clerk replies that this one is very special because it can talk. The shopper is impressed enough that he buys this special talking bird and takes it home. The very next day he returns, disappointed. "The bird didn't talk." The clerk asks, "Did he look in his little mirror?" "Little mirror? I didn't buy a mirror. Does he need a mirror?" "Of course," replies the clerk. "He looks in his little mirror and sees another bird in there. He thinks he's not alone and starts to sing. Starts to talk. Got to have a mirror." This sounds reasonable, so the customer buys a mirror and leaves. The next day he is back again, disgruntled. "The bird looked in his little mirror," he says. "But he still didn't talk." "Well," ponders the clerk, "Did he run up and down his little ladder?" "Ladder? Does he need a ladder?" "Of course," replies the clerk. "Don't you feel better after you exercise? When your little bird runs up and down his little ladder, those endorphins start pumping in his little brain. Makes him want to sing. Makes him want to talk. Got to have a ladder." "How much is a ladder?" "It's $12.95." "Give me a ladder." And off goes the customer. The next day he is back, with a scowl on his face. "The *bird walked up and down his little ladder. He looked in his little mirror. But he still didn't talk!" The clerk listens to the angry customer and then asks, "Did he swing on his little swing? You see, when the bird swings it makes him think he's back in nature. Makes him want to sing. Makes him want to talk." "How much is a swing?" "It's $7.95." The customer grudgingly buys the swing and leaves. But the very next day he is back again, angrier than ever. "The bird swung on his little swing. He ran up and down his little ladder. He looked in his little mirror. But he still didn't sing and he still didn't talk!" "Hmmmm," thinks the clerk. "Did he tinkle his little bell?" The customer doesn't even wait for an explanation. Determined to see this out to its conclusion, he grabs a little bell, throws some money on the counter and storms off. You guessed it—the next day he is back again. "The bird's dead!" he exclaims. "Dead?" "Yup. Dead. His little feet sticking up in the air. He got up this morning healthy as could be. He looked in his little mirror. He tinkled his little bell. He ran up and down his little ladder. He swung on his little swing. And then, just before he keeled over and died, he looked over at me, a little tear forming in his little eye, and he finally spoke to me. He said, "Didn't they sell birdseed?!" Let that story sink in for a moment. The Internet is full of dead and dying businesses that have been distracted by the bells and whistles of technology. They've ignored the lesson of the birdseed! So, what is the "birdseed" of marketing? We learned a few of the secrets in the last chapter. 1. Find a school of hungry fish! Once you've either found a lake teeming with hungry fish (or developed your own lake), your very next critical task is to 2. Discover what bait they're biting on. Given just these two advantages plus a plain-vanilla Web site, you'll run circles around 10,000 other eye-popping, flash-enhanced, multimedia'd, neato-bonito, techobrilliant, venture-capitalized, overhead-sucking, cashburning Web sites. But here's the problem. As more and more fishers discover the Internet, the fish are becoming more discriminating. Not only is the competition becoming more fierce, but the variety of bait these fishers use is* *staggering. In his excellent book, Differentiate or Die, Jack Trout (fitting name) has this to say: In 1987, there were 14,254 new products introduced in the United States, according to the reporting firm of Market Intelligence Service Ltd. By 1998, the number had grown to 25,118. To put that number in context, it means sixty-nine new products surfaced every day of the year.* Each of these new products has to be introduced and advertised, which means more fishers (competitors) with more bait (marketing messages). Eventually ordinary bait won't do. Your message will get drowned out unless you convert your ordinary bait into—superbait! 3. Convert your bait into superbait! The third most important skill of a marketer is to make your bait stand out from all other bait. The importance of differentiating your marketing message from that of your competitors was first defined in 1960 by an advertising agency chairman named Rosser Reeves. He called it the unique selling proposition, or USP for short. He taught that every advertisement must offer the customer a specific, unique benefit—a proposition that differentiates it from all other competitors. For example, look at the list of the following eight major companies and see if you can tell me their USPs. (You'll find the answers at the bottom of the page.) 1. Amazon.com ___________________________________ 2. BMW ______________________________ 3. Domino's Pizza ______________________________ 4. Federal Express ______________________________ 5. Mercedes ______________________________ 6. Nordstrom ______________________________ 7. Rolex ______________________________ 8. Volvo ______________________________ "Jack Trout with Steve Rivkin, D*

Companies spend millions finding, creating, and defending their USPs. What is your USP? Whatever it is, it must set you apart. It must make you different. Even after you've *found a school of hungry fish—even after you've discovered what they're biting on—your bait will get lost in the whirlpool of competing messages unless you figure out a way to make it stand out from the rest. Here is another excellent quote from Differentiate or Die: In 1966, Peter Drucker defined leadership when he wrote: "The foundation of effective leadership is thinking through the organization's mission, defining it and establishing it, clearly and visibly." Well, we're now in a new millennium and an age of killer competition. We would change only one word in that definition to bring it up to date: "The foundation of effective leadership is thinking through the organization's difference, defining it and establishing it, clearly and visibly.* I'm personally aware of the power of USP. It made me three fortunes and cost me another. In 1980, I published my first book, which has a powerful USP title—Nothing Down: A Proven Program That Shows You How to Buy Real Estate with Little or No Money Down. The companion to this book was a $495 weekend seminar by the same name. The power of this single discriminating USP leapfrogged my book and seminar past all other real estate books and seminars almost immediately. Although I was the new kid on the block, older and more established seminar outfits could not compete with my USP. They began to copy my Nothing Down message to market their own seminars . . . but it was too late. I had overtaken them and they never recovered. Later in the decade, new competitors (e.g., Carlton Sheets and Dave Del Dotto) usurped the lead from me when they used powerful infomercials to offer the No Money Down message on audiocassettes. I was slow to respond—stubbornly maintaining that the best way to learn was in a live seminar. I hadn't been listening to my "fish," who were eagerly snapping up the inexpensive home-study copycats. The allure of an audio program over a live seminar is that not only is it less expensive, it can be listened to over and over again. I had been leapfrogged! I closed down my seminar operations and went off to lick my wounds. A year later, I returned. Rather than fight the new leaders head-tohead, I* *set off in the opposite direction. By listening to the fish, I discovered that what people really wanted was not to listen to tapes, but to be taken by the hand and actually shown how to do it. More important, they would pay a significantly higher price for the privilege. Rising like the phoenix from the ashes of my previous business, I started offering indepth $5,000 Wealth Trainings—weeklong events with actual field exer-cises during which the students would buy real property. It was like playing Monopoly with real buildings. I had no competition. Over the next five years, our company taught over 20,000 graduates—bringing in over $100 million from these trainings. What was my USP? Hands-on, in-depth training. By focusing fiercely on this USP, we did extremely well for many years. Lately, I've uncovered and pioneered another USP. And it's hot! This new USP is based on the word mentoring and features live teleconferences—where real millionaires and multimillionaires actually mentor you in real time in the comfort of your own home.*

How Do You Create a Powerful USP?

Let's learn how to create a USP. The letters actually stand for the words
unique selling proposition, but let me show you how to supercharge your
USP—how to create a USP that not only differentiates but actually sells
what you have. I'll give you words to use as a hook to help you remember
the three most important aspects of creating a powerful USP:

Ultimate advantage
Sensational offer
Powerful promise

Ultimate Advantage

What specific benefit do people get from doing business with you that they could not get from one of your competitors? The very first and most important part of a USP is to give the customer a major advantage or benefit. Try to make each benefit something that none of your competitors offer—differentiate your product or service in at least one major way.

In 1873, a tailor named Jacob Davis in Reno, Nevada, was listening very carefully to his customers—mostly miners participating in the later stages of the gold rush. One frustrated customer found that the pockets of his work pants repeatedly tore out. In a flash of insight, Davis decided to strengthen the pockets and the zippers of his customers' pants with copper rivets. That solved the problem, and soon other customers were demanding the same alteration. Business was booming. But Davis was worried.

What if someone copied his idea? Lacking the $68 necessary to file for a U.S. patent he contacted the most likely potential partner, Levi Strauss,

the famous clothier who had been outfitting working people for almost 20 years. Strauss, recognizing the power of the idea, immediately joined in the patent application, which was granted on May 20, 1873. In 1872, Levi received a letter from Jacob Davis, a Reno, Nevada, tailor. Davis was one of Levi Strauss's regular customers; he purchased bolts of cloth from the company to use for his own business.

In his letter, he told the prosperous merchant about the interesting way he made pants for his customers: he placed metal rivets at the points of strain—pocket corners and the base of the button fly. He didn't have the money to patent his process, so he suggested that Levy pay for the paperwork and that they take out the patent together. Levi was enthusiastic about the idea, and the patent was granted to both men on May 20, 1873. He knew that demand would be great for these riveted "waist overalls" (the old name for jeans), so Levi brought Jacob Davis to San Francisco to oversee the first West Coast manufacturing facility. Initially, Davis supervised the cutting of the blue denim material and its delivery to individual seamstresses who worked out of their homes. But the demand for overalls made it impossible to maintain this system, and factories on Fremont and Market Streets were opened. Levi's simple copper rivet became not only the ultimate advantage but a legally protected advantage since the patent excluded all other clothing manufacturers from copying this revolutionary process. For the next 35 years, until the patent expired in 1908, Levi Strauss jeans became the standard for toughness in men's work clothing. It symbolized the individuality and strength of the American male for the next 100 years.

Can You Discover the "Copper Rivet" for Your Business! When designing your business, you need to lie awake nights trying to discover ways to separate yourself from all of your competitors. On the Internet you will be competing with people from all over the world. Why should anyone buy from you? What advantage can you offer that truly separates you from the pack? In other words, what single benefit do your customers get from you that they won't get from a competitor. Take out a package of 3 x 5 cards. Write on each card the words, "You get . . ." and then write one major differentiating advantage on each card.

Keep writing until you fill out as many of the 100 cards as possible. You should continually ask yourself this question as your business grows, because people can come along and steal your advantage. They may be able to copy where you've been, but if you keep improving your advantage, you'll always leave them in your dust. As an example, here are 10 of the advantages that I wrote on my 3 x 5 cards to describe the benefits enjoyed by those who are enrolled in my current millionaire protege program. 1. You get to be personally trained by #1 best-selling author Robert Allen. 2. You get to be trained in real time by a team of successful millionaire mentors. 3. You get to do this from the comfort of your own home or from any telephone in the world. (You don't have to travel to be taught.) 4. You get to brainstorm real case studies where you witness real, live, moneymaking success stories as they happen. 5. You get to ask interactive questions in an exciting real-time setting. 6. You get to be in the inner circle instead of being out in the cold. 7. You get to be part of a powerful network of millionaires-in-themaking. 8. You get instant connections by having access to the Rolodex of your millionaire mentors. 9. You get to have first access to the moneymaking ideas of your mil lionaire mentors. For example, your stock market instructor earned 400 percent on his money last year. When he makes a real-time trade, he will send an e-mail telling you what he is doing. You can watch him make money or emulate his winning trades. 10. You get personal transformation. There is a difference between information and transformation. I don't want to just teach what you need to know, but to transform your ability to act upon what you know. Once your list is complete, try to determine what your one major advantage is and then emphasize it in everything you do. Just make sure it is a unique benefit that only you offer. Each one of my 10 advantages is unique from that of my competitors—but one benefit is preeminent, the big kahuna, the major one. This is the one that I emphasize in all of my advertising. Can you guess which one it is? Over the years, this major advantage has shifted in response to competition. For example, here is how my major advantage has evolved over the years:In describing my ultimate advantage to my prospective proteges, I use this analogy: If I've done one thing right in my career, I've always searched out successful mentors to guide me. For instance, after graduating with my MBA in 1974,1 decided not to go the corporate route and chose instead to work with a multimillionaire real estate mentor at a much-reduced salary. What he taught me in those special six months transformed my life. In the next three years, using what he taught me, I myself was able to become a real estate millionaire. I shudder to think what would have happened to me if I had taken the other route. Then I decided to write a book about my experiences. I flew to Hawaii with my wife and baby daughter and pounded away on an old typewriter until I had an outline for the book I wanted to write: Nothing Down: A Proven Program That Shows You How to Buy Real Estate with Little or No Money Down. Rather than go the traditional publishing route, I approached a very successful best-selling author who happened to go to my church and asked her advice. She agreed to become my mentor and invited me to go with her to the annual booksellers' convention held in Atlanta that year. With her guidance, I had the courage to approach the president of Simon & Schuster, who recognized the value of my book and published it. It went on to become (and still is) the largest-selling real estate book in history. People ask me why I have been able to accomplish so much, and I tell them that it's all due to the quality of my mentors. Who is your mentor? If you're like most people, your mentors are your best friends. And that's the problem. According to one study, you can determine the income of an individual by adding up and averaging the incomes of his or her 10 best friends. Did you get that? Your income is the average income of your 10 best friends. If you want to double your income, what do you have to do? Get new friends! You need to add more successful mentors to your life—people who are earning 10, 20, 100 times what you are earning. How *else are you going to be able to see beyond your problems except to know someone who has a higher perspective? For example, when I wanted to learn about the stock market, I put out feelers to find someone who had been able to crack the market and could show me how to play the stock market successfully. When I found this individual, I said something like this: "I'm looking for a mentor to show me how to make serious money in the stock market. I don't just want you to tell me—I want you to show me. I'mnot interested in reading your books, listening to your tapes, or going to your seminars. I don't want you to sell me a treasure map to the gold mine you've discovered. I've gone that route before. And I've learned that after I've read the book, listened to the tape, been to the seminar, and studied the treasure map, I probably still won't understand how to do it. I'll spend the next three years studying and learning from the school of hard knocks. My three-year education will probably cost me about $20,000, and I still won't be any closer to where I want to be. So, Mr. Mentor, rather than my spending $20,000 and wasting three years of my life, why don't I just give you the $20,000 right now? You say you've discovered a gold mine. Let me go with you. Let's get in your pickup truck. Take me to the mine! Let's go down the mine shaft together. Show me the vein. I want to see it with my own eyes. Let me dig some out with my own hands. Don't tell me about the mine— take me to the mine! Now! And I'll make it worth your while." And that's what he did. We got on the phone and he took me live into the Internet and showed me exactly how to do it. I saw it with my own eyes. I could ask him questions. He gave me immediate answers. He was able to download his lifetime of experience into my brain in a few short weeks. Now I know how he does it. Just as my mentors have taken me into the mine, I want to take you into my mine. Would you like to come? Can you see how this analogy drives home and highlights my ultimate advantage? What is your ultimate advantage? Take time to figure this out at the beginning of your business and you will be much more successful. The second letter in the new USP formula is*

S, for sensational offer. Sensational Offer Do you recognize a good deal when you see it? Suppose you receive an offer to buy a music CD through the mail. The price is $20 but you can have it for only $16. Is that a good deal? Maybe. But in the same batch of mail is an offer to send you eight music CDs for only 1 cent! And if you check a little box on the order form you get another CD absolutely free. Nine CDs for a penny. Is this a better deal? Absolutely! And that is how Columbia House sold millions of music CDs. They hooked you on the front end with a sensational offer and then hoped to make it up on the back end with repeat orders. Such a deal! How to Create a Sensational Offer Everyone likes a deal, a bargain, a discount. There are ways to package a deal to make the purchase appear to be a bargain. The other day, while surfing for an airline ticket, I did some comparison shopping at several of the major online travel sites. All of the airfares were within a few dollars of each other, but one site included a 30 percent discount on a future ticket

from the same airline. This bonus did two things: It enticed me to buy from this site instead of the others, and it forced me to return to this same site the next time. It locked me up now and in the future. Smart. This little incentive tipped me over the top. The travel company was giving a volume discount: Buy two, get 30 percent off. It's a no-brainer. Have you ever watched a Ginsu knife salesperson at your local county fair? First, he demonstrates how sharp the primary knife is by cutting leather and a lead pipe. "How much is such a knife?" you're thinking to yourself. "Got to be at least 20 bucks." Then he shows you the fillet knife . . . which he uses to cut the skin off a tomato. Then there's that neat little potato slicer that cuts up a potato like an accordion. Got to have one of those! And then there's a special Orange Juicer. But wait! Have you seen this excellent paring knife? "How much for all of this?" he asks. "Just 20 bucks." Now he's got you. But wait, there's more. "If you buy right now, I'll give you another one of these large

Ginsu knives absolutely free . . . so you can give one to a friend." That does it! You're fighting all over each other to hand in your 20 bucks. My wife buys a set of these every year—just for the entertainment value. It's an unbeatable deal. It really is. You need to lie awake nights figuring out a classy way of offering special bonuses to go along with your main product to make it look like an unbeatable deal. Here are some examples of things you could offer a first-time buyer: An extended warranty A discount coupon.

A free special report A CD-ROM containing a free book or other valuable information A free banner ad on your site The goal is to reward your customers for taking action—to make each purchase a surprisingly pleasant experience. But don't stop there. In addition to giving them a bargain on the front end, you should build enough into your price to send them a "surprise" bonus with every purchase—to reward, delight, surprise, and astonish your customer for his or her purchase. Now, for the final piece of a powerful-selling USP. Powerful Promise The thing that clinches a deal is trust, and let's face it, with your first time buyer you don't have any. What is an instant way to gain trust? Offer a clear, unmistakable, no-questions-asked guarantee. But this isn't enough. You need to supercharge your guarantee with a powerful promise. You see, a guarantee by itself is powerful, but when you attach your guarantee to a powerful promise, you've supercharged it, you've energized it, you've made it real. The promise should heighten your uniqueness. For example, consider hotel room service. Any hotel can guarantee to deliver your meal quickly. But Marriott goes a step further: "Your meal in 30 minutes or it's free." Now that's a promise with teeth! It heightens and illustrates Marriott's USP of quality service. In promoting my previous book, Multiple Streams of Income, I made a bold promise: "If you haven't earned an extra $10,000 as a result of reading Multiple Streams of Income in the next 12 months, call the number in the book and I'll personally refund your money—and you can keep the *book as my gift." How can I make such a bold promise? Won't thousands of people rip me off and take advantage of my guarantee? Frankly, if a person reads this book and can't make an extra million in his or her lifetime, I wouldn't want their money. I'm not worried about the 1 percent of people who might take me up on my guarantee. I'm trying to convince the 10 percent who are sitting on the fence to get off and buy now. An Outrageous Promise In coming up with a powerful promise, you may need to push the envelope—get outrageous, take a risk. Then work backward to figure out a way to deliver on your outrageous promise. For example, in planning this book, I started with an outrageous question in my mind: "How quickly could someone launch a cash-generating Internet business from scratch?" Would it take a month? A week? A day? Half a day? None of these numbers seemed outrageous enough. Then I thought, "How about one hour—60 minutes? Hmmm. That sounds outrageous!" I reworded the promise to make it sound as dramatic as possible. How about this? Zero to Cash in 60 Minutes! Yes, that's it! Zero to Cash in 60 Minutes. Now that's a challenge that I could throw my creative juices into! There was only one problem. I had no idea how to do it. I wasn't even sure it was possible. But the more I mulled it over, the more exciting it sounded. I could see myself on a major radio talk show with a skeptical host. "Well, Mr. Allen. You say you can show our ordinary listeners how to make extraordinary money online. Okay, you've got an hour. Put your money where your mouth is—show us the money!" Then I imagine taking the host and the listeners through the step-bystep process of setting up a Web site, getting an e-mail address, and marketing a product or idea—and generating at least one cash order in 60 minutes or less. Would that be dramatic? Absolutely. Would that sell books? Absolutely. With this vision in my mind, I then proceeded to do the research to make sure that such an outrageous promise is actually deliverable. The result of that research is the book you are now reading.*

I'm sure this is the same process that a magician like David

Copperfield goes through in trying to create a new illusion to astonish and amaze an audience. He thinks to himself, "I wonder if I could make an elephant disappear? Or a Learjet? No, not dramatic enough. What about the Statue of Liberty? Hmmm. If I could make the Statue of Liberty disappear, that would be memorable!" Then, he works backward to pull off this illusion. What looks like magic to the audience is a carefully prepared illusion. It's not magic when you know the trick. In your marketing, I'm asking you to go through a similar process. What is your outrageous promise? For example, if your product is about weight loss, what outrageous promise can you make? How much weight could a customer lose safely and permanently . . . in how short a time? Then reengineer your entire company to be able to deliver on that promise. Let's review. The three powerful bedrock principles of Internet marketing success are as follows: 1. Find a school of hungry fish. 2. Discover the bait that they're biting on. 3. Supercharge your bait with a powerful USP. The letters USP, an acronym for unique selling proposition, also indicate how to supercharge your USP: Ultimate advantage Sensational offer Powerful promise If you discover and champion your ultimate advantage, if you create a sensational offer, and if you then back it up with a powerful promise, you will have done more for your business than 99 percent of all businesses in this country. In the next chapter, I show you how to whip your fish into a feeding frenzy for your product.

CHAPTER THREE

POWERFUL PRINCIPLES FOR CREATING A FEEDING FRENZY

In this chapter I show you how to get people to beg for your products—how to create a feeding frenzy with your marketing program. But before we go any further, let's make sure we agree on what marketing really is. Most people equate marketing with sales or advertising. It is much more than that. It starts with identifying the right audience (hungry fish). From your very first connection with a member of this audience, it continues on through every contact—from this person receiving a brochure to visiting your Web site to having a conversation with a live receptionist to the eventual sale and beyond—until your new customer is converted into a raving fan. Theodore Levitt, the famous Harvard marketing professor, said it this way in 1975: The marketing process consists of . . . "a tightly integrated effort to discover, create, arouse, and satisfy customer needs."*

In his excellent book, Permission Marketing," Seth Godin refers to the marketing process as one of converting strangers into friends and friends into customers. I go a step further on both ends of the scale. The marketing process should not start with strangers but with "starving strangers"—people who are predisposed to want what you have. Convert these starving strangers first into friends, then into customers. But don't stop there. Ultimately, you want to convert these customers into partners—loyal allies who profit with you in sharing your business with others. Figure 4.1 shows a visual representation of this process. As we learned in Chapter 3, first you identify a group of "starving strangers" and dangle your super USP bait in front of them. How can you get them to not only notice your bait but to actually strike it—to chase after it in a feeding frenzy? As a student of marketing for over 25 years, I have discovered some principles that always work. For more than 10 years, I practiced these principles without knowing that there was a scientific basis for why they work. Then someone gave me a copy of Dr. Robert Cialdini's powerful book, Influence: The Psychology of Persuasion. The lights went on! Cialdini gives detailed scientific proof explaining why certain marketing principles that have been practiced for millennia always seem to work. With this information, a marketer can design powerful marketing programs to take advantage of innate human tendencies. When I finished reading Cialdini's book, I was astounded. It reminded me of an old cartoon I saw in an ancient Bennett Cerf joke book in our family library when I was just a kid. Two lone Native Americans from New Mexico are standing next to a fire on a hill trying to send smoke signals when, across the valley, a giant atomic mushroom cloud appears. One Indian turns to the other and says, "Gee, I wish I'd said that!" While you're shopping on the Internet for one of my previous books (Nothing Down, Creating Wealth, or Multiple Streams of Income), you should also put into your shopping basket a copy of Cialdini's book. It is excellent. Here are Cialdini's six principles of persuasion: 1. Reciprocation 2. Commitment and consistency 3. Social proof 4. Liking 5. Authority 6. Scarcity

I used several of them in designing my marketing campaign for the Internet challenge. In order to demonstrate, let's return to my first two e-mails sent to my homegrown e-mail list of 11,516 newsletter subscribers. You might want to flip to page 17 in Chapter 2 and reread the first of these messages. This is actually a very sophisticated marketing message designed to create a feeding frenzy starting with the very first words in the subject line: "Making massive amounts of money on the Net." One-Step versus Two Step Process This is probably a good time to mention that your marketing campaign can be either a one-step or two-step process. In a one-step process, you try to go from an ad to a paid order in one step. For example, suppose you are an attorney trying to attract new business. You run a television ad that tells about your services and gives your telephone number. You are trying to go from an ad to an order in one step. This approach attracts only serious customers. It's like walking up to a total stranger and proposing marriage. This approach can work—if you talk to enough strangers, you're bound to find someone who is in the market for a spouse—but be prepared for a lot of rejection. A two-step ad offers the reader a free taste. Your ad doesn't sell your attorney services . . . but instead offers to let someone come in for a free one-hour consultation. You get people to raise their hand and indicate their interest in talking to an attorney. This approach attracts interested people while at the same time giving you a chance to talk to a more qualified group of people. Certainly, in a group of interested people, there must be some serious customers. In the marketing business, this is called lead generation, or getting people to raise their hands. To use one analogy, it's the dating approach. In our over communicated world, the two-step approach takes more time, but it is the best long-term approach. How do you get people to raise their hands? You have to give them something of value. For years, to market our popular Nothing Down weekend seminars, we would offer a 90-minute free preview. Over 2 million people attended these free lectures in the 1980s. I didn't know it at the time, but in offering this free seminar I was actually practicing two powerful persuasion principles explained so eloquently by Dr. Robert Cialdini: (1) reciprocity and (2) commitment and consistency. In lay terms, reciprocity means giving gifts. When you give gifts, people feel a subtle obligation to return the favor (to reciprocate). The entire Internet is based on reciprocity. Almost everything is free. But have you noticed that there are always options to pay for more personalized service? That is why, in the first of my five messages, I offer the possibility of winning some money. The opportunity to win money is given as a free gift. . . tapping into the power of reciprocity. Giving something for free is always a smart marketing strategy. Why do you think Debbie Fields gives free samples of her famous Mrs. Fields cookies? Everybody wins—the sampler and the marketer. Those who taste and don't like the taste haven't risked anything. Those who taste and want more can pay for the full treatment. The next of Cialdini's principles is commitment and consistency. In lay terms, this means baby steps. To use a bit of Eastern philosophy, "Man who chooses the beginning of the path also chooses the end of it." In his book, Cialdini reports on exhaustive research to prove that these small actions have a powerful effect on influencing a target audience to say yes. Cialdini calls it the power of commitment and consistency—if a person will take a baby step or make a small commitment toward a goal, he or she will be much more likely to continue. It's similar to the principle of inertia in physics—an object at rest tends to stay at rest and an object in motion tends to stay in motion. If you can motivate someone to take even a minuscule action, it is much more likely that he or she will continue to move in the same direction. In the first of my marketing messages, you'll also notice that I mention my new best-selling book. Why? Another important marketing principle is at work here—Cialdini calls it the power of consensus. In lay terms, this means popularity. If you see a long line forming outside a theater, you will automatically assume that the movie must be good. In other words, my book must be worth buying because so many people are buying it. People always want the hottest thing. If you can provide proof that your product is in demand by a large number of people, it will induce potential buyers to say yes more easily. Review that section of the e-mail and you'll see what I'm trying to convey. In both of the first messages, I also mention that Guthy/ Renker, the famous infomercial company, is shooting an infomercial with me. This builds credibility. People like to deal with experts. It lowers their risk of failure. Cialdini calls this the authority principle. In lay terms, this means credibility. You'll notice I use several methods of building credibility. Another important marketing principle is also at work here. You'll notice that I tell my readers exactly why I'm trying to make $24,000 in 24 hours. I'm not trying to hide or hoodwink. I tell readers that I'm trying to make money to document my infomercial—and I ask for their support. I tell the truth—straightforward and unvarnished. I can't overemphasize the power of telling the truth. Another very important part of my first e-mail message is using what Cialdini calls the power of scarcity. You'll notice that I say there will only be five messages, culminating with the final message on May 24. This highlights the very special, unique, and scarce nature of this promotion. I can't overemphasize the importance of the power of this principle. There is another example of scarcity used in this message. Can you find it? Again, in the second message (page 19) I return to the power of the principle of reciprocity by promising that each and every person who votes will receive a copy of a valuable ($100) special report. In a sense, I am paying them for the time they spend in filling out my survey. Other principles are equally as powerful. Here is my expanded checklist of 12 powerful persuaders, translated into simplified language: Principle 1 Giving gifts Principle 2 Baby steps Principle 3 Popularity Principle 4 Credibility Principle 5 Scarcity Principle 6 Honesty Principle 7 Rapport Principle 8 Urgency Principle 9 Greed (pleasure) Principle 10 Fear of loss (pain)

Principle 11 Belonging Principle 12 Curiosity To help you remember the most powerful of these 12 principles, I've boiled them down into the three most important, never-miss ways to supercharge your bait. Once again, the acronym USP appears. Urgency Scarcity Popularity Question: If a lot of people are competing for a few items with a short deadline, what do you have? Answer: Feeding frenzy! Now that you are more aware of these principles in action, let's study the third message, sent a few days later. Notice how the future feeding frenzy is being set up.

CHAPTER FOUR

The Secret to Online Streams of Income

Traditional Marketing Snail mail (slow, expensive, unreliable, wasteful) High mailing costs Long delivery time Business week/business hours Local/limited geographic area Limited, shrinking customer base High overhead Real time, real contact Average customers Long inquiry time Dress up/go to the office Mass marketing Impulse/wait Old, traditional Intrusive marketing (interrupts) One-way marketing One-dimensional marketing Ads disappear quickly High entry costs High cost of failure Operate from a fixed location Need to be a big player with big money High barriers to entry Highly visible/public You are judged by age, sex, $, looks, race Uncool Internet Marketing E-mail (fast, cheap, reliable, efficient) Zero mailing costs Instantaneous delivery time 24/7/365 Entire world Unlimited, expanding customer base Almost zero overhead Store-and-forward time (asynchronous) Upscale, wealthy, intelligent customers Instant response time Stay home in your T-shirt Intimate, one-onone marketing Impulse/instant gratification New, exciting, mysterious You're in the searching mood (welcome) Interactive marketing Interactive and multimedia marketing Ads are as permanent as you want

Low entry costs/level playing field Low cost of failure Operate from any computer in the world Can be a nobody with little or no money No barriers Private/anonymous between buyer and seller Judged by the quality of your ideas Cool

That is quite a powerful list of advantages! The most important thing you should take away from reading such a list is the revolutionary nature of these advantages. Internet marketing is turning traditional marketing on its ear. In Chapter 3 I shared with you Jay Abraham's three major marketing activities: (1) to find more customers who will (2) spend more money (3) more often. The Internet is a perfect vehicle for magnifying these three activities for one major reason: the free nature of frequency. In other words, your marketing message can be delivered over and over again with almost zero cost. In my $24,000-in-24-hours Internet marketing challenge, I was able to deliver five long, powerful marketing messages to the same audience for free. What a marketing luxury! If I had tried to replicate this marketing effort in the bricks-and-mortar world via direct mail, it would have cost me at least $25,000 up front, without knowing if I could recoup my costs. Internet marketing is much more forgiving because the cost of failure from a single marketing message is zero. Did you get that? In the bricks-and-mortar world, the cost of a marketing failure can bankrupt your company! On the Internet, because of the advantage of free frequency, you have the ability to build your message to a powerful crescendo. Now, let's study the fifth and final message from my Internet marketing challenge. It was sent on May 24 at exactly 12:38 P.M. As I've previously mentioned, the response was overwhelming. Money started to pour into my e-mail box within minutes and gushed to almost $100,000 in just a little over 24 hours. Read it and see if you can tell why.

Over the past 14 days I have sent you four separate messages announcing a special promotion on May 24. THAT'S TODAY! (To read these four messages, click on the link below.) Today, as I sit at my computer, I want to thank you for participating in this experience. In these past few days, over 2,000 of you have responded to our survey, and hundreds of you have sent friends and associates to register for the free Streams of Cash E-Letter. As a reward for participating in this Internet challenge: —Three of you will be randomly selected to win CASH prizes! —Three of you could also win CASH for referring someone! —Three of you will win $500, $250, or $100 for making a guess! —The first 100 guessers will win a signed million-dollar bill. —The best 100 guessers will win a signed book. —2,000 of you will receive the powerful special report: How to Make $24,000 Cash in 24 Hours on the Internet And EVERYONE who orders TODAY becomes an INSTANT WINNER because I'm going to make some once-in-a-lifetime deals TODAY ONLY! Why today? Because, we are making history TODAY! As I send you this message, live cameras are rolling to document how you can make instant CASH on the Internet. As the responses to this message pour in, our staff will total up the number of orders. I want to make sure that the end result looks impressive. That's where you come in. Let me ask you ... Do you really want to be a millionaire? In the past few months, Regis Philbin has helped three people become millionaires on the hit show, Who Wants to Be a Millionaire. Through my books, seminars, and trainings, I have helped thousands of people become millionaires.

And now it's your turn. When would you like to get started? How about now?!!! There are three ways I can personally help you become a millionaire: Package #1. Millionaire Mentoring conference call: Eight weeks of intense telecoaching with me and my hand-selected Millionaire Mentors. Package #2. The Millionaire Retreat: Three powerful days of personal interaction with me and my handselected Millionaire Mentors. Package #3. The Inner Circle: Two days of intense, personal coaching with me (strictly limited to 10 individuals). Each of the above methods comes with many valuable bonuses. But first, let me ask you: How would you like to receive your millionaire training? —By telephone with live Millionaire Mentors? —At a private Millionaire Retreat, where you can network with other likeminded people? —With a handful of individuals, where you will receive personal, face-to-face mentoring? Each way is a different experience that I guarantee you will enjoy and profit from.

First, every attendee at the Millionaire Retreat will be allowed to participate in the Millionaire Mentoring conference call (package # I) AT NO CHARGE. Here is what the Millionaire Retreat consists of. In the survey, the most popular offer BY FAR was this three-day Millionaire Retreat. Half of those surveyed were willing to pay between $500 and $ 1,500 per person. Over 100 people were willing to pay $ 1,495 per person. This is far below my normal price of $3,000 for a three-day session like this— considering that I will be bringing in at least five millionaires to teach the session with me. But since I'm filming this offer for the live television cameras, I want to guarantee a huge response. Therefore, for 24 hours ONLY I will allow you AND your spouse to attend for an unbelievably low price. Over 20,000 people invested $5,000 apiece to participate in my powerful 5-Day Wealth Training. From this class have come hundreds, if not

thousands, of millionaires. I have designed a more concentrated three-day version of this training called the Millionaire Retreat. During these three intense days you will learn: How to earn 100 percent or more in the stock market! You will be trained by an expert who himself earned over 400 percent last year in the market. How to moke $100,000 *a year investing in real estate. You will be trained by at least three real estate millionaires in addition to myself. Learn the inside secrets to making huge amounts of money in real estate. How to make $1,000 a day or more on the Internet. The Internet is the ultimate money machine ... while you eat, while you sleep, money is pouring into your life from all over the world. Let me show you how to really make money on the Internet. How to build inner wealth and unshakable confidence. Most people want to be successful but lack the inner confidence to break through to new levels of success and achievement. Using powerful new brain technologies you will be able to transform your ability to take action. How to build a financial fortress around your assets. People ask me if I'm a millionaire, and I say absolutely not. And neither should you. Let me show you how to shield your wealth using strategies that I have never before revealed. You will be trained by myself and my team of millionaire mentors. These three days are guaranteed to change your life forever and launch you on the fast track to financial freedom. If you can't attend, the entire experience will be professionally recorded. All attendees will also receive a copy of the tapes. As bonuses, every participant in the Millionaire Retreat will also receive: 1. Everything in package # I FREE OF CHARGE 2. A FREE ticket for your spouse/partner to attend with you 3. Real estate millions home-study system Enjoy live recordings from two of Robert Allen's popular programs on how to make a fortune in real estate. Attendees paid $5,000 for each of these seminars. Now you can learn the same information that helped launch thousands of millionaires. The Wealth Training Experience 12 audios Fortunes in Foreclosures 24 audios 4. Infopreneuring: Be an information multimillionaire! In the past 20 years, over $200 million worth of my books, tapes, videos, and seminars have been marketed throughout the world. I shared the secrets to how this was done in a powerful three-day $3,000 seminar* *called "Infopreneuring: How You Can Become an Information Multimillionaire." You will receive a live audio recording of this exclusive information marketing boot camp with 24 audiocassettes. 5. Special bonus: You will also receive two tickets to the Internet marketing boot camp, June 16-18. The tuition for this class is $597. I have made an arrangement with my friend, Carl Galetti, who is organizing this conference, to pay your tuition for you. That's right, your tuition to attend is zero. If you can't make these dates, then give the two tickets to someone you know. They will love you forever. I myself will be there. I wouldn't miss it. And neither should you. If you would like to read about all of the incredible bonuses available to attendees of this conference, just click on the link below. Then you'll see why this bonus alone is worth the entire cost of the Millionaire Retreat. So, to review, the Millionaire Retreat includes three days of powerful training for you and your spouse, plus: Everything in package #1 A free ticket for your spouse/partner to attend with you 36 audiocassettes on real estate riches 24 audiocassettes on infopreneuring millions Two tickets to the Internet marketing boot camp And all of this for three easy payments of $297. Your satisfaction is absolutely guaranteed. I guarantee that you will learn the ideas, strategies, and techniques to launch yourself to the next level of success.*

Many of you are serious Internet marketers who could benefit from the traffic that I am generating on my site. In the survey, over 1,000 of you indicated that you would like to buy a banner on the Multiple Streams of Income site; 61 people offered $995 for the privilege. Obviously, there is a huge demand and a high value for this very limited space. Therefore, rather than placing a price tag on this scarce resource, I'll let you place your bid for what you feel this *would be worth to you and I'll accept the 24 top bids. The 24 winners will receive five specific advantages. You get a banner ad on the front page of my popular Web site linked to you. I have never before allowed banner ads on my site. Yet in the next several weeks I will be driving massive traffic to my site with 500,000 pieces of mail, constant PR as I go from city to city promoting my new book, and, of course, over 30 references to my Web site in my best-selling book. If you need traffic, here is a perfect vehicle. Choose any four-month period you wish. You also receive an exclusive positioning for your ads in one of 24 places throughout my site. 1. In addition, you will be able to place 10 classified ads in the soon-to-beopened Money Classifieds. 2. You will also receive a prominent, endorsed ad in each of four issues of the Streams of Cash E-Letter. 3. And you'll receive professional advertising consultation worth $500. I'm sure you want your advertising to be as effective as possible. Therefore, I have arranged and paid for a professional marketing expert, Scott Haines, to professionally critique your banner advertising. Scott is my own personal marketing specialist. He normally charges $500 per marketing consultation. However, for this special promotion, I've purchased a block of Scott's time and brainpower for him to supercharge your advertising. Scott is a pro. I myself have hired Scott to help me with several of my marketing campaigns—with great success. I'm impressed with his work, and I know you will be. He will give you powerful suggestions on how to double the response to your advertising. Repeat: This consultation is available at no charge to you. I have already paid the fee for you. 4. You will also receive a four-week Internet action class. Let my personal Internet guru, Daren Falter, coach you via conference call for four power-packed weeks. He'll show you how to make millions on the Internet. Bonus: Two tickets to Internet marketing boot camp, June 16-18. Read all about it at the link below. The tuition for this class is $597. I have made an arrangement with my friend, Carl Galetti, to pay your tuition for you. That's right, your cost to attend is zero. If you can't make these dates, then, give the two* *tickets to someone you know. If you would like to be one of the 24 people, click on the link below and make your bid. If the results I achieve in the first month don't meet my expectations, I reserve the right to cancel the remaining months of my bid. Well, there you have it. Four powerful ways I can help you become a millionaire. Click on the link below to choose your package number, fill out your name, address, and credit card number, and send it off immediately. Robert Allen Author of the New York Times best-sellers Nothing Down, Creating Wealth, and Multiple Streams of Income.*

Now you have had a chance to read all five messages sent over a period of 14 days, just for fun, which of the four offers I made in the last message attracted you the most? I'd like you to vote, and then I'll show you on the next page how many people voted with their wallets for each option. Your vote ______ Package #1. Millionaire Mentoring conference call $97 ______ Package #2. Millionaire Retreat 3 payments of $297 ______ Package #3. Inner Circle 3 payments of $997 ______ Package #4. Banner advertising Your bid $ ___ In all, 173 people either made bids or cash offers for one of the four packages. The following tally includes all additional orders that came in after the 24-hour deadline. This is a response rate of 1.5 percent . . . three times what 1 expected.

Package # 1. 83 people paid $97 $ 8,051 Package #2. 42 people made 3 payments of $297 36,531 Package #3. 17 people made 3 payments of $997 50,847 Package #4. 29 people made bids 19,478 Miscellaneous 3 people ordered individual products 597 Total orders $115,504 Over the next three months, after cancellations, we were able to *deposit over $90,000 in cash orders, with a profit of almost 90 percent. You're probably asking, How can I duplicate this?! That's what this book will show you. In fact, I want to show you how to do even better, because I learned a lot from this experience. But before I teach you the duplicable systems for consistently creating these kind of cash flows, let me dispel a myth that I'm sure a few of my readers have picked up along the way. It's the get-rich-quick mentality that pervades business. I, too, am guilty of it. Remember, I'm the guy who promises to show you how to make money in 60 minutes starting from scratch. This gives the impression that I'm only about the quick buck, a thoroughly American pastime. Therefore, I refuse to go any further without clearing up this misunderstanding. Just as a bee is lured to the nectar of the flower, businesspeople are lured to money. Honeybees accomplish so much in their relentless search for nectar—they pollinate the flowers and bring about glorious growth wherever their industrious bodies carry them. Entrepreneurs are the honeybees of our economy. They are attracted to money and freedom, but along the way they spin off a growing economy with jobs and knowledge and charity. I am proud to be a honeybee in the hive of capitalism. Ultimately, the goal of any entrepreneur is to extend the life of his or her enterprise for a lifetime. In this sense, the short-term goals of making money now collide with the long-term goals of creating an enduring enterprise with endless cash flow. Therefore, your marketing plan on the front end must emphasize immediate gratification. But the back end of your marketing program must emphasize a deepening relationship with the fish in your hatchery. Here is where we part company with traditional mass marketers, whose traditional mass-marketing dream is as follows: Send out a million emails. Get a 1 percent response on a $100 product. Collect a cool million dollars. Ride off into the sunset. This is the mass-marketing model—or what I call "going wide." Mass marketers cast a wide net, hoping to get a tiny percentage to respond and make millions. It would seem as though the Internet is perfect for the mass-marketing* *model. It is. But remember with whom you are competing. The Fortune 1000 companies are spending, on average, a million dollars per Web site to go online. Do you have a million dollars to make your site look snappy and exciting? Don't even go there. Remember, it's not about the quality of your Web site. In the future, with billions of people online and hundreds of millions of competing businesses from Argentina to Zanzibar, you will never be able to compete on price. People will be able to search the world to shave a penny. Once again, don't go there. There is only one way you will be able to compete and create lifetime streams of cash flow for yourself: Go deep. What does that mean? It means that you anoint yourself as the in-depth expert on what your starving crowd wants and create a deepening relationship with them—a lifetime relationship. As the relationship deepens, they will pull from you more and more products, services, and information (PSI) at increasingly higher and higher prices—because price will not be the issue. When a stranger in Kathmandu tries to push a product that is 10 percent cheaper, your fish will think of the benefits of their relationship with you and quickly reject the stranger's offer. How do you create this kind of relationship? It starts with a new attitude about marketing. After you find your hungry school of fish, you must resist the almost universal attitude to focus on selling products. As a businessperson, your ultimate product is a satisfied customer. Over 25 years ago, Theodore Levitt published a powerful article in the Harvard Business Review titled "Marketing Myopia." Even though you may not have read it, I'll bet you've heard some of the analogies that he used to make his point. He clearly showed that the railroad industry declined rapidly from its zenith because its leaders thought they were in the railroad business (product-centered) when they were actually in the transportation business (customer-centered). Because of this myopic view, they didn't even consider the advent of the airplane important. Not only did they miss out on the opportunity, they almost got wiped out by it. The same thing happened to the movie industry when television came on* *the scene. Why did this happen? Here are a few of Levitt's conclusions: In short, if management lets itself drift, it invariably drifts in the direction of thinking of itself as producing goods and services, not customer satisfactions. . . . The historic fate of one growth industry after another has been its suicidal product provincialism. . . . The entire corporation must be viewed as a customer-creating and customer-satisfying organism. Management must think of itself not as producing products but as providing customer-creating value satisfactions. It must push this idea (and everything it means and requires) into every nook and cranny of the organization. . . . In short, the organization must learn to think of itself not as producing goods or services but as buying customers, as doing the things that will make people want to do business with it.* In the May 31, 1999, issue of Business Week, Jeff Bezos, the CEO of Amazon.com voiced the same sentiment, almost as if he were reading from the same text: We want to be the world's most consumer-centric company. . . . We focus incessantly on trying to get the customer experience right. . . . See, we're not a book company. We're not a music company. We're not a video company. We're not an auctions company. We're a customer company. You might be wondering why I'm delving into theory and philosophy after all this intoxicating talk about making big money in 24 hours or less. The reason I've been able to earn a large amount of money is because of my relationship with my customers. They trust me. I try not to abuse that trust. When I talk, they listen. This trust has taken me 20 years to establish. I am customer-centric, not profit-centric. I want my students to win—to succeed. As you create your business, your most powerful tool is trust. Abuse that trust for a quick buck and you undermine your long-term business. Your customers will tolerate only so much abuse before they swim off to someone else's pond.*

Now that you understand the importance of going deep, you might appreciate the framework of techniques and systems that you can put in place to perpetuate your business. Use Jay Abraham's marketing materials as a primary source; I have created a template in Table 5.1 for you to keep TABLE 5.1 Summary of Jay Abraham's Marketing System 12 Ways to Increase the Number of Leads 9 Ways to Increase Your Closing Ratio 3 Ways to Decrease Attrition/Increase Retention 6 Ways to Increase Size of Your Average Order 6 Ways to Increase the Frequency of Purchase 1 . Referrals 2. First order at cost 3. Guarantee or risk reversal 4. Host/ beneficiary relationships 5. Advertising 6. Direct mail 7. Telemarketing 8. Special events and seminars 9. Use qualified lists 10. Unique Selling Proposition 11. Client education 12. Public relations 1 . Increase selling skills of your entire staff 2. Listen to best books and tapes 3. Model your best salespeople 4. Get a sales manager 5. Go out and get sold — model your competitors 6. Qualify leads up front 7. Make ads specific, not general 8. Make irresistible offers 9. Educate your customers 1 . Call inactive customers to get feedback 2. Give extraordinary service 3. Communicate! 1. Up-sell and cross sell 2. Point-ofpurchase promotions 3. Bundling/ packaging of complementary products together 4. Increase your prices and enhance your margin 5. Change the profile of your products to be more upscale 6. Offer larger units of purchase 1 . Develop a back end 2. Continuous communication 3. Endorse other people's products to your list 4. Run special/ private/closeddoor sales 5. Program your customers; educate them into a longterm buying strategy 6. Use price/ purchase inducements like frequentflyer miles

in front of you as you make major marketing decisions. It outlines the following: 12 ways to increase the number of leads Nine ways to increase your closing ratio Three ways to increase retention and decrease attrition Six ways to increase the size of your average order Six ways to increase the frequency of purchase Jay is a close friend and personal mentor from whom I have learned an enormous amount *about marketing. In an extraordinarily generous move, Jay has made his complete marketing manual available for free over the internet. Go to www.freemarketingbook.com and download this powerful 246-page PDF-format book directly to your hard drive. A thousand people paid $1,000 apiece to get advance copies of this material. You can now have it for free. What a bargain. A lifetime of marketing wisdom in minutes. I highly recommend it. Join me in the next chapter to learn seven powerful ways to drive traffic to your site.*

CHAPTER FIVE

Powerful Ways to Drive Traffic to Your Site

"It's the marketing, stupid!" Blunt. But true. It's not about having a fancy Web site. It's about the marketing. It does no good to have a Web page if you're the only one who knows it's there. Nobody is going to stumble onto your site by accident. Unless you do something, nobody is coming to check you out.

There are six major ways to attract people to your site. I've already eliminated buying one-minute spots during the Super Bowl. Not because it's expensive but because it's monumentally stupid. It would be like trying to warm the homeless with bonfires of real money. We're going to do the smart thing and start on a shoestring. If it works, we'll do more of it. If not, we'll have money left over to try something else. In this chapter we learn six major ways to attract traffic to your lonely site: 1. Building your Web presence 2. Search engines 3. Free and paid ads in the online world 4. Free PR in the online and offline worlds 5. Paid advertising offline 6. Word of mouse Some of these ways are high-leverage. Some are low-leverage. By leverage I mean the ability of your marketing efforts to produce multiple, massive, and residual exposure. If possible, you want the effects of your marketing to reach huge numbers of people, multiple times, over a long period of time. By contrast, some of your marketing activities will reach only a few people one time—and then the message is dead. I always think more clearly when I have a big-picture representation of the overall task I'm trying to accomplish. Figure 6.1 shows an illustration of the six major lakes of potential customers. Starting with this map, we're going to tap into each of these six lakes of potential prospects to drive traffic to your site. On the high end of the leverage scale is the use of search engines, because one well-structured placement can be seen by millions of surfers over and over again. On the low end of the leverage scale is handing out your business card to a single person, who might just throw it away. We'll start with the lowest-leverage option because this is where most people start. The Importance of Building Your Web Presence If you're going to play online, then act like your life depended on it. Tell everyone you know about it. Embed your Web address and e-mail address in your offline brochures, on your business cards, in every marketing message, and in every advertisement you place. Put it on a bumper sticker, in greeting cards, and in wedding gifts. Put it on your answering machine message. I mean everywhere.

Create a signature file to attach to every e-mail that you send. In fact, if you haven't done it already, open up your favorite Web browser and add a marketing message to your e-mail messages right now. Your message should be a short marketing message that directs people to your Web site. Every click counts. I'm using the Internet Explorer browser, so here is how I add a signature file to my e-mails: Click on Tools, then Options, then Signatures. Compose a message to be added to the end of every e-mail you send. In addition to these obvious ways of getting your message out, here are five more ways to make your Web presence known.

1. Go to www.usenet.com and join any newsgroups related to your subject. Post messages in appropriate places. 2. Become an opinionated expert at epinions.com 3. Lurk in chat rooms. 4. Participate in bulletin board discussions. 5. Register your freebies at a "free stuff" site. Look around the Net for sites that promote free stuff. Contact these sites and offer some of your own promotional goodies. Taking Full Advantage of Search Engines Here is a cardinal rule of marketing: Inbound marketing is much easier than outbound marketing. In other words, it is much easier to make sales when customers are calling you than when you are calling them. Cold calling is hard because you are interrupting people when they are not in the state of mind to buy—they're probably in the state of mind to have dinner. But when customers call you looking for a solution to their problem, they are in the state of mind to buy. They are interrupting you. (Don't you love to be interrupted by a hungry prospect?) It's the difference between reading an ad in a newspaper versus one in the Yellow Pages. If you're looking in the Yellow Pages, it's most likely because you are actually searching for a solution to your problem. The sale is already made in your mind. You're just shopping for the right price, availability, and relationship. Which kind of prospect would you like? An angry, interrupted customer or an anxiously seeking customer? Give me the Yellow Pages kind of customer all day long—except for one problem. It costs money and requires a long-term commitment. Now let's go online. Although there is an actual Yellow Pages online, the traditional form of online searching is through search engines such as Excite and/or directories such as Yahoo!—big companies with big computers will help you search for exactly what you want. The best part is that the vast majority of these searches are free for both parties—the advertiser and the searcher. What a deal! Suppose you wanted to use the Net to research ways to create traffic to your Web site. Where would you start? First let's research a list of the top search engines. Go to www.goto.com and enter the words "top ten search engines." Scanning down the list of search results, you find a listing similar to the following:

The Major Search Engines and Directories Summary of the major search engines summarized, with historical background and reasons why each is important to Webmasters or users. www.searchenginewatch.com You click on the underlined link and after a few minutes of perusing you find a current list of top search engines and directories in alphabetical order. AOL Search (for those on AOL) AltaVista.com Askjeeves.com DirectHit.com Excite.com FASTSearch.com Go/Infoseek.com Google.com GoTo.com HotBot.com IWon.com LookSmart.com Lycos.com NorthernLight.com Raging S earch. com RealNames.com Yahoo.com WebTop.com You go down the list and click on the link to Excite.com (because you like the sound of it) and enter the word traffic in the search box. Once again a gargantuan computer scans the entire world and brings back a list of . . . well, as of this writing . . . 2.93 million references to the word traffic . . . almost all of them referring to automobile traffic. Nope. That doesn't do us much good. So you refine your search and include the words "Increasing Internet traffic," hoping to narrow the search down a bit. Now there are 9.53 million references! Here is what happens when you search at some other top search engines:

Search Words Traffic Increasing Internet Traffic Lycos 10,832,107 163,047 AltaVista 7,554,731 77,603 Northern Light 5,151,479 204,897 Are you beginning to see the problem with search engines? How can you search through a million pages? You can't. So you settle for the first 20 on the list. That leaves millions of other pages out in the dark. If you can figure out a way to be among the top 20 listings, you might attract a traffic jam to your site. If not, it's like finding a needle in the biggest haystack on planet Earth. Impossible. Still, most research shows that the vast majority of people online begin their searches using one of the top search engines. Here are the facts: Fact: Over 80 percent of Internet users use search engines to find information. Fact: A typical search can often generate thousands, if not millions of results. Fact: Only those Web sites listed in the top 100 will ever see any significant traffic.

Fact: Each day, millions of online businesses are competing for those top 100 spots. Fact: The odds of little ol' you and me being listed in the top 100 are slim. Still, there are ways to improve your odds. So you must try . . . if only to understand what the fuss is all about. And who knows, maybe your product, service, or information is unique enough to give you a very rare search engine word that cuts competition to a small number. Therefore, you have three choices: (1) Do it yourself; (2) hire someone to do it for you, (3) pay for traffic search engines. Do It Yourself Surf to the site of every major search engine, read the submission guidelines, and manually submit your Web page and cross your fingers. Before you get started, however, you would do well to check out these three Web sites for tips on how to increase the chances of your success: www.

searchenginewatch .com www.searchengines.com www.bruceclay.com For the do-it-yourselfer, there's an excellent book on the subject by Ken Evoy. It costs about $20. You have to download it from his site at www.sitesell.com. It's exhaustively detailed, and I guarantee that you will learn things you never knew. If you'd like some software that will help you with your manual submissions, go to www.searchengineconimando.com. And here's another service to help you track your position on the major search engines: www.wpgold.com. Frankly, the do-it-yourself approach, although time-consuming, is certainly less expensive and will give you a nuts-and-bolts feel for the inner workings of the Internet. Hire Someone to Do It for You If you want to search out a never-ending list of companies that will help you submit your Web page to every search engine and directory in the known universe, just go to any search engine and type in free search engine submission. Excite.com lists 1,865 references. You should find plenty of sharp companies in the top 20 to help you. After all, if they have been able to get themselves listed in the top 20 while competing with almost 2,000 companies, they must know something about what they're doing.

Hi, my name is Shawn Casey and I'd like to show you around the world of pay-for-traffic search engines. In addition to the free search engines like Yahoo!, several search engines allow you to actively bid for positions under search terms. When someone searches for a specific term, the listings show up in the order of highest bidder first, second highest bidder second, and so on. If two companies bid the same amount, the first bid gets priority for the listing and will be listed first. You pay only when someone clicks on your listing and is delivered to your Web site. The most prominent of these search engines is GoTo.com. Others include Kanoodle.com and RocketLinks.com. For explanation purposes, I'm going to focus on GoTo because it's the largest and best-developed pay-per-hit search engine. Similar sites have less traffic, but *you often pay less because not everyone uses them like GoTo. GoTo's motto: "It's targeted, cost-per-click advertising and you set the cost per click!" Two basic concepts apply to using these types of search engines to your best advantage: 1. While you obviously want to pay the least possible amount for each hit you get, you're going to have to bid more if you want a higher listing and, therefore, more traffic. You have to carefully track the traffic you get from the search engine so you know the value of that traffic. If you don't know the value, you could be paying too much for your traffic or missing great opportunities to generate more traffic for a higher price. In other words, let's assume you're selling an item with a $25 profit margin. If 1 percent of visitors to your site buy the product, then each visitor is worth 25 cents to you. If you can draw traffic for less than that, you're making money on each sale.*

2. The other concept involves bidding for several hundred keywords at low prices (e.g., a penny apiece). This way you are listed all over the search engine. Each keyword by itself won't bring much traffic, but the total may be 100 or more hits per day. If you're only paying a couple of pennies per hit for this traffic, then it should be profitable for you. If you search popular words like business, you'll find that the cost of being number one is quite high and the position is usually held by larger enterprises such as Inc. or Entrepreneur magazines. Large companies are often willing to invest millions of dollars in building their brands, so they'll pay more for traffic than it would normally be worth. I strongly suggest you don't compete with them unless you are absolutely sure your business model will justify it. Often, you'll be able to find a top-10 ranking for a third or less of the price of being number one. Since you're limited to buying only traffic that's profitable for you, this position will probably suit you better. Even if you end up far lower in the rankings, your investment must stay within an appropriately profitable range. You'll probably get less traffic than the *number one ranking, but it will be traffic you can make money on. That's far more important. Here's how to use GoTo. The other search engines will work in a similar fashion. 1. Create an account with Go To. To start your account, you must register with GoTo and post a balance of $25 or more. Without this account, you can't submit bids. When someone clicks on one of your listings, GoTo will charge the expense against your deposit. When your balance gets low, you simply deposit more money. Since this is a prepaid plan, you have complete control over how and when you spend your money. There's no risk that GoTo will be sending you a large invoice at the end of the month. You spend only as much as you want on advertising. 2. Determine the value of a visitor to your Web site. You can do this for Web site visitors in general or for specific sales promotions in particular. The value may vary by keyword. The simple formula goes like this: Divide the average number of new customers each month (a period long enough to be statistically significant) by the average number of monthly visitors to get the percentage of visitors who actually become customers. If you multiply this percentage times your average profit margin on sales to new customers, you get a good idea of how much a visitor is worth to you on the first visit.*

For example: If I average 10,000 visitors per month to my Web site and sell a product with a $20 profit margin to 150 customers, then I can easily calculate the percentage (150/10,000) to be 1.5 percent. Multiplying 1.5 percent by $20 yields $0.30, which is the value of each visitor. It's interesting to look at the bigger picture of this example as well. While making $0.30 per visitor doesn't seem like much, the dollars grow quickly when you multiply pennies by thousands of visitors. My profits for the month with 150 sales would be $3,000 less advertising costs. If I can generate visitors at $0.10 each, for a total cost of $1,000, then I have a profit of $2,000. Since, in our example, $0.30 *is the maximum value of a customer to the Web site, we'll use $0.30 as the maximum we would bid for any search term. Why would we give up all the profit to get a customer? Presumably, your business plan includes the sales of additional products and services to your newly acquired customers. Even if you break even on the acquisition of these new customers, you should be able to make a profit on additional sales to them. This is why it's important to understand the lifetime value of your customers. 3. Develop an extended list of keywords for your site. Keywords are any terms related to the content of your Web site. You'll want to make this list as extensive as possible. If you are selling computer software, you'd have a list like this: Computer Software Microsoft Html Quicken Games Corel C+ Intuit C++ Spreadsheet Clip art Word processor Excel Front page Lotus Your list will contain a lot of words only marginally related to your site and, often, not high-volume search terms. You want these terms because the bidding for them is usually much lower than for a comparable position under software. You'll get less traffic from terms other than software, but that traffic can be very profitable for you. You don't have to pluralize your search terms. The search engines will automatically do this for you when a visitor is searching the terms. To maximize your success, you'll want to eventually develop a list of at least 1,000 keywords. You don't have to use that many to get started. In fact, you'll probably want to start with 15 or 20 until you get used to the system. To derive the most traffic, however, you need to use as many search terms as possible. If you're wondering how you're going to manage such a huge list, read on for the relatively simple solution. In fact, this is also how you'll get the least expensive traffic. You'll bid only a penny or two for 90+ percent of your extended list. If you bid a penny on 900 terms and average one hit per term per day, you get 90 hits per day for $0.90. Since you only have to set up the bids once, you can continue to generate traffic like this for quite a while after investing the initial time and effort. GoTo offers a tool that provides suggested search terms. For instance,* *if you are checking out travel, the system delivers 100 or so related search terms you might want to add to your list. 4. Develop a title and a description to be used with your keywords. When the search engine users get the result of a search, they'll see the highlighted titles for each listing followed by a short description. You should think of this as a classified ad with a headline and short copy. The keys to your success here are as follows: • Use an attention-getting headline to get as many people as possible to read the description. You want to be sure to use important, proven, and successful terms like free and you. • Write a description that succinctly tells the reader why he or she would be a fool not to click on your link. For most keywords, this is the best plan because you're paying only a penny or two for the clickthrough. But, you'll want to be more selective about the copy for the more expensive bids. If you're going to pay a quarter for each clickthrough, then you may want to have higher-quality traffic. You don't want just anyone to click through. You want people who are likely to buy. How do you limit traffic to the higher-quality people? Your description for the expensive bids must provide sufficient informa tion for the reader to determine whether your site/offering/prod uct/service will really be of interest. For example, you wouldn't want to use a teasing phrase (e.g., "learn how to get free software prod ucts") when you're paying a lot of money for prospects. • You can direct each keyword to a separate page on your Web site (although you probably won't want to target 1,000 entry pages), so you'll probably want a separate description for each entry page. • You should have the ability to track each entry page so you can determine the success ratios of click-throughs to sales. I like to do this for high-priced keywords even though GoTo will allow you to*

use its own system to track click-throughs. It's nice to be able to double-check your results. • Test, test, test. You'll take your best shot with your first posting. You should always be testing to see if you can improve the response. Remember, this response can be improved in two ways. The first is by the quantity of click-throughs. The second is the quality of the visitor because higher sales ratios mean greater profitability. 5. Place your bids. GoTo's DirecTraffic Center is the account management tool you'll use to add, modify, or delete your listings. Since this is the Internet, you can use the DirecTraffic Center day or night. After you've set up your account, you can log in to the DirecTraffic Center. You have two choices of ways to enter your listings. The first method is to manually type in each separate entry. The second method is to create an Excel spreadsheet and simply upload the entries all at once. Assuming you're starting out with just a few entries, you can manually enter those. In the long run, especially with your list of over 1,000 keywords, you'll want to use the spreadsheet option. Using Excel will allow you to work offline as you enter all of your information into the spreadsheet. Then, you just e-mail the file to GoTo. After a review, GoTo will load the information for you. If you have the Microsoft Office Standard, you have Excel on your computer. You don't have to figure out how to use the program to create a spreadsheet from scratch. GoTo provides a template that you can download and fill out. All your keywords and descriptions must be reasonably related to the content of your Web site. GoTo's staff reviews every submission and will refuse listings that are not on topic. When you submit your spreadsheet with hundreds of search terms, you'll have to do a tremendous amount of research to determine how much to bid for each term. As an easier option, just bid one penny for every term to start. In the next step we'll talk about how easy it is to manage your bids so you can adjust the important ones later. 6. Reevaluate and adjust your bids. At the DirecTraffic Center, you can modify your bids on all your search terms on the fly. If you determine that the traffic generated by a specific keyword is more valuable to you than other keywords, you can go online and immediately raise your bid for that term. You'll instantly increase your traffic. Sophisticated users of GoTo will even track patterns showing which days and times generate the most sales from GoTo traffic. During this prime time, they will raise their bids to increase traffic. As soon as the slot ends, they will lower their bids to the old levels. Currently, GoTo searches return 40 listings on the first page. If you're on this page, there's a chance that the searcher will see your listing. Accordingly, your goal is be listed in the top 40 whenever possible. As you refine your GoTo listings, you'll find yourself jockeying for position on certain pages by raising or lowering your bids by a few cents according to what others are doing. For busy search terms like travel, a penny might buy a listing only on page 6, number 203. You're unlikely to get much traffic from this position. You might find that it's worth spending 10 cents to move up to number 75, for example. If you could afford to pay the dime, you'd most likely get a lot more traffic. Here are the links to some pay-for-traffic search engines: www.GoTo.com www. RocketLinks. com www.Kanoodle.com That's a brief overview of the pay-for-traffic search engines. I want to thank Shawn Casey (www.shawncasey.com) for being our tour guide. Now, let's explore how to buy advertising online. Free and Paid Ads in the Online World As a marketer, your goal is to create an online business that is scalable. (I thought I'd drop one of those trendy Internet words to impress you.) Scalable means the ability to grow from small to large quickly. The essence of scalable is an old-economy word: control. What if you build a huge business that depends entirely on search engine traffic . . . and someone bumps you off the front page. Poof. There goes your traffic and your business. I don't like the sound of that—do you? No, I want a business where I can control the amount of leads that flow in. That means I need ready access to . . . an expanding source of hot leads from interested customers at a price that is not exorbitant—hopefully free. Search engine traffic, although mostly free, is outside your control. Unless you want to hire a full-time employee or two to constantly fight and jockey for top search engine placement, you'll need to find other sources of leads for your business. Just as in the offline world, you'll need to advertise. And you'll need *to pay money. And this is a problem because the models for effective advertising on the Net are still in flux and probably will be for years to come.We're just learning what works and what doesn't. For several years, banners were the hot thing until click-through rates dropped. What will be the next hot thing? At present it appears to be the pay-for-traffic search engines. On the horizon are several models where you pay people for reading their e-mail. The following are ways to obtain free or paid advertising online, listed in order of least effectiveness. Free Classifieds Have you seen ads on the Net that boast of placing your classified ad on 7,000 Web sites for free? The old adage, "you get what you pay for," certainly holds true in this case. Let's say it's worth a shot (which is what people say just before they plunk down some money for a lottery ticket). That doesn't hide the fact that the odds against winning are astronomical. Just in case you're so inclined, here are three links to free classified ads. www.buysellbid.com Millions of fresh classifieds every day. Easy to use. www.freeclassifiedlinks.com Free reciprocal-links newsletter that features high-quality Web sites that want to exchange links with you! www.classifiedclub.com Links to over 7,000 places on the Web where you can place a classified for free; costs you $29.95 to find out; but probably worth it. Banner Ads A banner is a rectangular box filled with advertising (and often fancy graphics) that you see displayed as a masthead on many Web pages. Go to www.cnn.com and see which banner ad is running right now in the top center of the page . . . then click on various pages at the CNN site and notice how the banners change. Somebody is paying for those banners, just as people pay for full-page ads in magazines or for commercial spots on TV programs. The hype about banner ads is that people can quickly click on the banner ad and have their questions answered immediately. The reality is that the click-through rate from banner ads is abysmally low. If you're paying good money, make sure there is a very solid tracking mechanism that enables you to determine the exact cost of a click-through and how many click-throughs result in an actual* *sale—so you can calculate your advertising cost per sale. If you search the Web, you see many advertisements for banner exchanges. For a fee, and sometimes for free, you can arrange to have a banner that links to your site placed on dozens, hundreds, and maybe thousands of other Web sites worldwide . . . with the hope that somebody,*

somewhere will see your banner advertising, click on it, and be transported to your site. Here are three free-banner-exchange sites. www.bcentral.com www.bannerexchange.com www.bitsonthewire.com Links to Symbiotic Sites A close cousin to the banner-exchange concept is to exchange links between your site and other sites with complementary (but hopefully not competing) products or services. A site that sells guitars might link to a site that sells guitar sheet music and vice versa. These links could be free or revenue-sharing, whichever works for your win-win negotiation. Here is one place where you can learn how to set up link exchanges. www.linkleads.com E-Zine Ads A much more targeted and effective strategy is to buy (or exchange) an advertisement in one of the thousands of regular e-zines that are published on the Net. Here your ad is read by a wide audience interested in your subject generally—similar to a full-page ad in one of the national magazines or newsletters. This can be an extremely good method for creating trackable, scalable, reliable traffic to your Web site. Here are two directories of major e-zines and how to contact them about buying advertising space in their targeted list of periodic communications. www.lifestylespub.com Run a complete, targeted ad campaign for as little as $150. www.freezineweb.com Tells how to place a free ad in over 200 e-zines. If you're trying to find an e-zine on a specific topic, go to www. ezinesearch.com. There will be much more on this strategy in later chapters. E-Mail Rental Lists Finally, as in the offline world, it is possible to rent names for targeting your e-mail marketing. The advantage, of course, is that you *don't have to pay for postage, which is usually the largest cost of any bricks-and-mortar direct marketer. One of the leaders in renting e-mail names is www.postmasterdirect .com. Using double opt-in standards (i.e., visitors are asked twice whether they wish to subscribe), Postmaster Direct maintains millions of names and rents them out to various businesses at anywhere from 10 to 30 cents per name. The company handles all of the e-mails, the merge/purge, and the details of the mailing. And you get the result.*

Of course, if you own a business that operates offline, it's only natural to want to move your business online. Over 99 percent of the Fortune 1,000 companies have already established an online presence. It would be foolish not to. But what if you own an exclusively online business? Is it smart for a small but growing online business to invest some of its marketing dollars in offline advertising? I'm not referring to buying expensive image-building television ads. The question is, are there ways to effectively advertise your Internet business offline? If you have a fixed budget, should you risk some of that budget in the offline world to drive traffic to your site? Your answer is determined by two factors: the quality of your message and the potential for finding hungry fish offline. The Quality of Your Marketing Message In other words, does your online advertising work? These new dot-corn start-ups, flush with IPO cash, blow unconscionable amounts of money on cute, hip promotions that don't attract real customers. When you're starting on a shoestring, you don't have the option of luxurious advertising. Every dollar must produce an increased return on your investment or you're out of business! Experts have often said that one of the greatest causes of small-business failure is running out of money. I disagree. I think that often the cause of small-business failure is too much money—- and wasting that money on ineffective marketing. I like marketing that must make a profit. It forces you to get real about what you say. Let me put it this way: Suppose you *were down to your last $1,000 and had to buy advertising that would not only return your $1,000, but would produce an extra $1,000 in sales so you could continue to advertise. Suppose the life of your business depended on placing the right kind of ad in the right place—if you succeed, you stay in business; if your ad is a bust, you close the doors. It would focus your thinking, wouldn't it? Before you make your final decision, don't you think you should do a little free testing first? Place 20 or 30 free classified ads with various headlines to see which one seemed to pull the most leads? Before you rolled the dice, wouldn't you try to refine your offer, add some bonuses, give a great guarantee—and then bounce that message off several thousand people to see if they would be willing to vote with their wallets? Or would you place your last $1,000 and the future of your business in the hands of some kid who just graduated from college with a degree in advertising? Sounds silly, doesn't it? Yet that is what happens every day in millions of businesses.*

Before you go spending a dime anywhere, you'd better test whether your message works. Start small and ramp up to larger and larger advertising expenditures online as your ads consistently produce a profit. Maybe then you might start the entire process over again in the offline world . . . with paid classifieds in appropriate publications, small ads at first, and then some targeted direct mail. If your advertising money produces a profit, then invest more money. And I emphasize the word invest. I'm railing against small-business people who rush into advertising to build market share, worried about other competitors moving in. Face it, you're not Amazon.com. Your company will look a lot better come IPO time if it has real cash flow, real profits, and real business. As my partner, Tom Painter, says, Keep it small and keep it all.

Finding a School of Hungry Fish in the Offline World

The cardinal rule we learned in Chapter 2 was to start with a hungry school of fish and feed them the bait they are biting on. Where do you find such hungry fish? Start with the Standard Rate & Data Service (SRDS), which offers a multivolume publication (found at most larger libraries) of information about how to advertise in almost every possible advertising medium. I recommend using the library version because getting your own subscription costs hundreds of dollars per year. If you're so inclined, there's a wealth of information at www.srds.com. Before you spend a dime in advertising, take time to ask yourself some serious questions about your target fish: What kinds of magazines do they read? What organizations do they belong to? What kinds of neighborhoods do they live in? What newsletters do they subscribe to? What radio stations do you think they listen to? Where do they play? Where do they go to church? Try to picture your ideal customers. Wander through their houses in your mind and notice what kinds of problems they are grappling with. What kinds of cars do they drive? Where do they shop? What kinds of credit cards do they carry? How would they like to hear about your message? What message would they like to hear? What solution are you providing to improve their lot in life?

Then you can scan through the SRDS volumes and track down the newsletters, the magazines, and the media outlets that might cater to your customers. Get a copy of the newsletters (if they allow advertising); buy a copy of the magazines and look at the ads that compete with your product. Notice the kinds of words they use, the kinds of offers they make, the kinds of hot buttons they push. Start small. Craft your message as if your life depended on it. Place a small ad and track the results like a wolf tracks a herd of caribou. If your ad produces results, you can increase your budget until you are running full-page ads in every magazine in the country. Before you reach that stage, you would do well to contact reputable list brokers from the Yellow Pages in your city to find out whether they have lists of prospective customers to whom you could send a targeted mailing for your product or service. Do the numbers to see whether, after deducting the costs of mailing and assuming a response rate of Vi to 1 percent, you would have a chance of breaking even. Your list broker can help you determine the realistic costs of a direct mail campaign. If the numbers seem reasonable, you'll have to either write a direct mail letter or hire someone to do it for you. An excellent software product that will help you write both online and offline marketing letters is found at www.instantsalesletters.com. To repeat, start small. Test a few lists. Measure the results and, if warranted, roll out your direct mail campaign to larger and larger numbers. The Power of Word of Mouse There are two final concepts in creating massive traffic: 1. Viral marketing 2. Affiliate programs These concepts are so important to the future of your business that I am going to devote several chapters to them (Chapters 8 and 11). In short, the concept behind word of mouse marketing is to enlist your customers to help you spread your message. In the real world, word of mouth is a potent source of advertising. Online, word of mouse is the most highly leveraged kind of marketing because people can communicate with each other so rapidly. A positive buzz can virtually launch your idea overnight. A negative buzz can kill it instantly. Don't miss the chapters that talk about this subject. Now, let's review our six strategies for driving traffic to your site. 1. Expanding your Web presence 2.

Search engines 3. Online ads 4. Public relations online and offline 5. Offline advertising 6. Word of mouse Take another look at Figure 6.1. The flow of money starts with the Great Ocean of Fish through six major sources of targeted leads. With your marketing activities you try to attract interested people into your Maybe Lake. Some of these Maybes flow into your Yes Pond by becoming customers. Eventually, a few of these special customers migrate into the Whale Pool and become partners with you in spreading your message.

CHAPTER SIX

How to Write a Press Release

A press release announces your website to the world. Also known as a news release, it should be informative and appealing to reporters and other contacts. State why your company or product or service is beneficial to people. Describe how your site or company was developed. Keep in mind that you are going to send your release to people who have hundreds or thousands of releases to read through. Make your company stand out with a well-written press release. Your priority is to please the editor/writer. When you write your press release, make sure you consider how your material could catch the editor's eye. Write an untraditional piece; include new angles that make your release stand out from the rest. If possible, find out about the editor or the audience of the magazine or newspaper where they work. Publication is more likely if you appeal to the current interests of the specific publication and the specific editor/ writer. Editors consider the demands of their audience. If your work fails to meet subscriber needs, the story will not be published. Keep your writing timely and be truthful. This will increase your chances of publication. Going Local: Let's face it, most websites will not get significant attention from large publications on a national or international level. If you have not done anything highly innovative or of interest to the big-time publications ... you

still have a shot at going local. Local and regional publications have a "local boy/girl does good" story and you don't need to be in the realm of rocket science or devising a plan for world peace to get local attention. Personalize your work and, whenever possible, emphasize the local angle, especially for small-town papers. Web, Brick and Mortar: Don't forget to also tell local customers where to find your business off of the Web, whether you have one location or several branches. Be consistent to gain a good reputation. Mislead your audience and it will backfire. You need to gain trust, so keep your information factual. Once the editor becomes familiar with your company name, he or she will be more inclined to publish your releases in the future. Submit your work on a regular schedule, and if you plan on resubmitting the same story to any another medium, inform the receiving parties. Find out what times are less hectic before you return calls to editors or reporters. Remain in good standing and the rest will take its course.

Lay-out... Press releases should generally be one or two pages in length, double-spaced and typed with 1.5- to 2-inch margins. Use company stationary that includes your logo and slogan, but avoid bright or dark-colored paper. Center the words News Re/ease before you begin writing. Under this header, type Re/ease after: and the date when you want your information made public. Include an exciting title that reflects the purpose of the release. At the top of the second page, type page 2 and follow with your logo and slogan so that the format is similar to the first page. (Leave out the Release after and the date that you typed on the first page. Everything else should be the same as your first page.) When your release is completed, type -30- or # # # (a way of saying the end) on the bottom center of the page. Information to include... Newsworthy information is best presented in the form of an inverted pyramid. This means that the first part of your release should be the key information. Answer the primary questions first, making sure to include any vital who, what, where, when, why and how elements. Their order is based on which elements are of greater importance to your particular news release. Elevator Pitch: Entrepreneurs in Silicon Valley seeking investors talk about the elevator pitch. They imagine being in an elevator with a venture capitalist or angel investor. They have only 5 or 10 floors to explain their business concept and attract the interest of the temporarily captive audience. You can think about the first (and maybe second) paragraphs along the same lines (except you don't have the luxury of a captive editor). Go straight to the point in the beginning because you hopefully will have time to explain later—that is, you will have time to explain in subsequent paragraphs... but only if you pique the interest of the reader in the first paragraph. Begin your release by making the news clear. The main focus of your first section is, "This is what it's all about." Information that supports or clarifies details in your release comes later, in the second part. Secondary information includes background information or any other details that you need to explain. Because less emphasis is put on this section of the release, get straight to the point and keep it simple. Keep the inverted pyramid format in mind, putting less important information lower in the release. The last section should include information that closes your release in a smooth but strong way. Don't leave people hanging, but, on the other hand, don't drone on and on. What does your company offer? How might people already be familiar with your company's name? This is the time to establish a connection for people between your website and company name. What else to include in your press release: 1. Enticing headlines which summarize the material that follows. 2. Follow a problem/solution format in your writing. (Also try com paring and contrasting ideas.) 3. You may want to include photos. Make sure that they are your own or that you have express permission. Make sure that they directly relate to what you are promoting. No stock images! You may also put photos for downloading from your site's press section. Include both black & white and color and a variety of resolution sizes. Magazine and newspapers have varying requirements. Note: Cover letters aren't necessary unless you want press coverage of a company event. Where to send your Press Release: • Appropriate writers @ magazines • Appropriate writers @ newspapers • Trade journals in your company's industry • Print magazines specific to new website announcements • Online agencies (optional)—they will distribute your release for a cost Note: If you select an online agency, make sure they are reputable. There are companies that either fail to distribute your release effectively or, even worse, fail to distribute it at all. Don't assume everyone wants an e-mail. Though it might seem to be the easiest way to send your release, take the time to develop separate contact lists of reporters who prefer e-mail, fax or snail mail (the kind that involves a real stamp and envelope.) Tips for Your Press Release • Don't send out mass e-mailings. • Don't hassle contacts by asking them if they received your release.Do the work yourself. Editors won't publish anything sloppy or hard to read. Make your news sound like news, not a sales pitch. Do research. Send releases only to editors who are likely to be interested. Don't be careless. Factual/spelling/grammatical errors make your site and company less credible. Only one news release per envelope. Mail release by first class if possible. Typing your address directly on the envelope is an impressive bonus (versus the use of labels).

Hiring Help for Press Releases

If you choose not to do the writing yourself, you can hire a freelance writer or public relations firm to create your news release. Keep in mind that it's important to thoroughly evaluate whomever you hire. Look in the yellow pages under "Public Relations" to find contacts. Interview candidates and ask to see published samples of their work. Whether or not it's a popular writer or firm, if they aren't getting releases published, they can't help you. See what they can offer you.

*Look for writers and firms that promise you publication in newspapers or other targeted publications. Not only do they have confidence in their work but they have the connections to get your release to the public. You have several options when considering a writer. Local reporters not only have the experience of writing for a targeted audience but they can often promise you publication in the newspaper or magazine where they work. Ghostwriters write news releases for you but make it appear as though you wrote it yourself. Other writers will represent your business by being the contact for the media. If you choose the second option, make sure the writer is responsible and familiar with your company.**

CHAPTER SEVEN

SIX MAJOR WAYS TO MAKE MONEY FROM YOUR SITE

Your Web page is the portal through which you will attract multiple streams of income into your life. Some of these streams will be gushers. Some of them will be tiny rivulets—mere trickles of cash flow. What makes these income streams possible is a steady stream of people. No people, no money. What I said in my previous book about the Internet is truer than ever: If you want to make money on the Net, having your own Web page is just the beginning. It's like having a billboard in the middle of the Nevada desert. . . if nobody sees it, it's as if it doesn't even exist. It's worthless. If the three key passwords in real estate are location, location, location, then on the Internet, they're traffic, traffic, traffic. Your most important task is to drive traffic to your site. If you have no traffic, your site has no value. I repeat: A Web page is nothing. Traffic is everything. By traffic, I mean visits by people. The more visits, the more valuable your space. Think of it this way: Before Las Vegas became the "hot spot" it was nothing but a few lonely buildings in the middle of the desert. Along came gambling and attracted a few people. The casinos needed to attract more people, so they added famous entertainers and glitzy

dancing girls. Traffic increased. They offered cheap airfares and inexpensive food. Traffic increased even more. They staged major boxing bouts, and people flew in from all over the world. Traffic increased again. They added a major convention center. Traffic zoomed. Then they added attractions for kids and families. Traffic exploded. With traffic flowing (people circulating) throughout the city, everything else in the city became more valuable . . . the commercial street corners, the office space, the restaurants, the retail stores. Newspaper ads, magazine space, billboards, television and radio spots—all increased in value. However, if the traffic were to stop flowing, the buildings would stand empty, the stores would have no customers, the population would leave. It would become a ghost town. Your Web site is like an imaginary city in the middle of the desert. If you can attract people to it—traffic—and encourage them to come back again and again and bring their friends, then everything on your site will increase dramatically in value. You own all the real estate—the digital property. You own the commercial corners, the malls and shopping centers, the residential apartment buildings. You own the television stations, the radio stations, the newspapers, and all the billboards on every street corner. Without traffic, all of these assets are worthless. With traffic, you can rent out these assets for a fortune! It's all about traffic. In Chapter 6 we learned six strategies for building traffic. In this chapter, let me show you how to build an Internet marketing machine—a machine that not only drives traffic to your site but gets people to leave money as they're passing through. Interested? Think of your Web page as a convenience store. Joe Customer walks in with the sole purpose of buying a gallon of milk. On his way to the coolers, he grabs a box of donuts. At the cooler, he remembers that he also needs some orange juice. Walking back toward the cash register, he spots some batteries. At the cash register, he adds some breath mints. He came in to buy one thing and leaves with five items. These impulse buys make up a large percentage of the profit of that store. Don't forget the main purpose* *of your site! All of your traffic-generating activities have one purpose in mind—to entice your visitors to sign your guest book and give you permission to contact them again. If you don't accomplish this simple goal, you have failed to build up an asset that will generate your prime source of long-term wealth. I know you want to make money now, but before you sign up for a hundred affiliate programs, stop and make sure you have accomplished your most important task. By gathering their e-mail address, you have introduced potential customers into your Maybe Lake—a reservoir of interested-but-not-yet-committed customers. Once you have obtained permission, you should send an immediate autoresponder e-mail congratulating your prospects on their wise decision and rewarding them with special goodies for reading your first message to them. I call this an ethical bribe. You are rewarding them for granting you permission to contact them. In other words, you are paying them for paying attention. In addition to gathering the e-mail address of every visitor to your site, let's explore the many ways you can induce your Web visitors to leave money. There are at least six main streams of income. Profit Center 1: The Main Product of Your Site After you have gleaned permission to continue to communicate with your prospects, the next most important task is to satisfy their primary reason for visiting. Something in your advertisement attracted them. They're interested in your offerings. During this very first visit, you may have only three clicks' worth of time to convince your curious strangers to linger long enough to find something they want. You should design a first-time buyer's reward—a package of incentives that tip the scales toward a yes rather than a no, as in the Chapter 3 example of discount airline tickets. If all the tickets are priced about the same, I'll go for the one that gives me the extra discount. What can you come up with that differentiates you from all other options? Could it be a gift certificate for a book or some other valuable premium? Could it be a coupon for a huge discount on a future order? Could it be frequent-flyer miles? Could it be a bundle of free reports? Could it be placing your customer's name in a monthly raffle to win one of your catalog items? Could it be a telephone consultation with you about the customer's area of interest? Could it be free placement of a classified ad in your newsletter or on your Web site? If possible, try to make the value of your first-time buyer's gift equal to or greater than the value of many of the items in your catalog. Remember, if you treat customers right, they will be back again and again . . . with an increasing volume of purchases. You need to invest in your customers so they'll invest in you. And that brings us to the second stream of online cash flow from your Web site.*

Profit Center 2: Joining Affiliate Programs

The Web is teeming with affiliate programs, the most famous of which is Amazon.com. The Amazon.com link has been added to hundreds of thousands of Web pages all across the Internet. Each of these links represents a minipartnership between the site owner and Amazon.com. The host site (Amazon.com) agrees to pay the referring site (you) a small fee to provide a link on your site to Amazon.com. If someone clicks on the Amazon.com link on your site and ends up purchasing anything, you will receive a commission for that referral. There are now hundreds of thousands of satellite partners who have an ongoing self-interest in the continuing success of the Amazon.com mother ship. I start with Amazon.com as an example because this strategy is one of the prime reasons for its incredible growth in gross revenues. The more affiliates the host site has, the better for spreading the message. Copying this successful strategy are thousands of other businesses marketing a myriad of products, all of which are trying to accomplish the same goal: increased traffic and thus increased business. Eventually, you, too, will want your own affiliate program to market your own products through hundreds or thousands of partnering sites. But before you launch your own affiliate program, you need to experience what it is like to participate in several affiliate programs. In Chapter 11, we will explore how to find and profit from the top affiliate programs on the Net. Online Affiliate Programs versus Traditional Network Marketing Programs Similar to affiliate programs are network marketing opportunities. They operate on the same model—a referral fee for steering someone to an existing business. But network marketing has more complicated compensation plans that reward you more extensively for the efforts of people recruited into your organization. Because of this extra layer of complexity and the extra effort required to build and maintain a growing downline, I highly recommend that you participate in only a single, excellent network marketing opportunity. Both affiliate programs and network marketing companies base their existence on the concept of rewarding people for their positive word-ofmouth advertising. Have you ever been to a great movie or a great restaurant and told a friend? That's called word-of-mouth advertising. Businesses love word-ofmouth advertising because it's more effective than all the money they spend on any other form of advertising, promotion, or marketing. Network marketing is a way for businesses to leverage the power of word - of-mouth advertising. Let me give you a hypothetical example. Suppose you recommend a great restaurant to your sister. Let's call it Chez Bob. Your sister and her husband make a reservation for dinner, and during the meal, the waiter asks them how they heard about Chez Bob. They mention your name. How would you feel if the owner of the restaurant sent you a thank-you letter and a coupon for a free meal in appreciation for your recommending his restaurant? It would probably make you feel wonderful. The restaurant owner also explains in the letter that because of your recommendation, Chez Bob has gained a new long-term customer. This customer didn't come as a result of a Yellow Pages ad or a radio and newspaper campaign. Therefore, he wants to reward you for this new word-of-mouth customer. Any time your sister visits his restaurant in the future, he will send you a check for 10 percent of the value of the meal as a continuing thank-you. Sure enough, every several months you receive a small thank-you check. You're so impressed that you encourage others to visit Chez Bob. This generates more free-meal coupons plus more 10 percent word-ofmouth checks. After a year, you are receiving several small checks a month. After several years, you've helped to create dozens of monthly customers that generate hundreds of dollars of extra, no-hassle income to you. That would be nice, wouldn't it? This is the theory behind network marketing, as it is now called. I prefer to call it relationship marketing because it is as a result of the relationship that word of mouth derives its power. Businesses these days spend up to 50 percent of the price of their goods for advertising and marketing expenses. Instead of sending these advertising dollars to wealthy newspapers, magazines, and television stations, several smart businesses have begun to share this money with their best customers. Every time one of their best customers influences someone to buy products, they send this loyal customer a check as a sort of referral fee. Eventually, these residual income streams flowing from dozens, hundreds, thousands, even tens of thousands of customers can become substantial (as in my personal case). But, as I said earlier, it takes time, dedication, and commitment to build substantial network marketing income streams, so I recommend that you choose only one network marketing opportunity and focus on it until you are successful. While I know of many people who earn income from a variety of associate programs, I know of no one who has successfully built and maintained more than one network marketing business simultaneously. In other words, pick a company and stick with it.

Profit Center 3: Opening Your Own Bookstore

No matter what your product is, you are ultimately in the education business. Your customers need to be constantly educated about the many advantages of doing business with you, trained to use your products more effectively, and taught how to make never-ending improvement in their lives. Each of your regular e-mail newsletters should be designed to continue the education process. Therefore, each e-zine becomes content that goes into your archives. Each detailed question you answer in your e-mail becomes a template for the Frequently Asked Questions (FAQ) section of your site. Eventually, the content from your FAQs and e-zines will end up as a series of special reports (which can be combined into a full-length book), which you can either sell or offer as a premium bonus in your marketing efforts. What should you offer in your bookstore? The following four major items: 1. Your own special reports 2. Your own books 3. Resource materials from joint-venture partners 4. Your own selection of traditionally published books The fastest way to stock your bookstore with books is to become affiliated with a major online bookstore (more on how to do this in Chapter 9). You can display on your site your own private selection of books that pertain to your industry or product line. It stands to reason that if a person is interested in your product line, he or she should also be interested in any related information. Why not profit from this special interest? The disadvantage to this approach is that (1) profits earned from these minor sales will be minimal (3 to 7 percent of the purchase price), and (2) it drives traffic away from your site, perhaps never to return. A more profitable alternative is to research self-published authors online who have created information content that would be suitable for your visitors and arrange to buy their information products on consignment. The price you can charge for such content is generally higher, with correspondingly higher profit margins, and you don't have to lose the traffic to Amazon.com. Of course, the highest profit margins are for information products that you create yourself, such as books and special reports. If you plan carefully, a series of special *reports can actually be organized into a full-length book, Dr. Jeffrey Lant, in his impressive book, How to Make a Whole Lot More Than $1,000,000 Writing, Commissioning, Publishing and Selling "How-To" Information, reveals that one of his most powerful profit centers is the creation of five-page special reports. He sells each special report for $6 (three of them for $14). Rarely does anyone order fewer than three at a time. In the back of his book he lists over 100 of these special reports . . . and I defy you to read through the list and not end up wanting a half a dozen for yourself. What is so incredible about these reports is that they can be created from recycled material such as your FAQs and newsletter articles, thus providing an ongoing cash infusion to your business. Here is what Lant says about profitability. Special Reports are very profitable. Because people tend to buy in multiples of three, Special Reports have become a very important profit center for me. No wonder. Consider the cost. Direct costs include the value of my time in creating them (which may mean recycling material from other sources) or getting other specialists to create them for me. . . . Factoring all expenses, including postage, the individual Special Report costs about 45 cents to produce. I sell them for $6 without any problem.*Of course, Lant's book was written in 1993, before the Internet really exploded. The costs associated with digitally producing and delivering a special report have now been reduced to almost zero! Lant boasts that he creates 24 to 28 of these five-page special reports per year. (The magic number of five pages keeps the postage down to one first-class stamp.) Each report is personally individualized with the purchaser's name and current date. Another benefit of creating these special reports is the publicity value. To quote Lant again, Let me share a secret with you. Special Reports actually have two names. I call them Special Reports when I sell them to individual buyers. And I call them articles when I offer them without charge to editors and publishers for immediate publication. Nothing else is different; you need make no changes in the actual title or content for the different* *markets. These special reports can become the basis of your PR campaign. Submit them as is to newspapers, magazines, and e-zines to help spread your message. Each special report should include a resource box at the end, with details about how to reach you for more information (for a fee, of course). Your special report becomes a sophisticated marketing vehicle. In time, your resource center can become one of the most profitable profit centers on your entire site. Now for the next source of site cash.*

Profit Center 4: Advertising In an analogy at the beginning of this chapter, I described how Las Vegas was converted from a desert ghost town into a thriving metropolis because of the traffic flowing through it. Where there is traffic (i.e., eyeballs), there is the potential to rent this traffic to other businesses. People want to rent these eyeballs, and other businesses will pay you up front for that privilege. The downside is that these eyeballs may be siphoned off to another part of the online universe, never to return. Of course, your eyeball asset has no value until you have enough eyeballs to make a difference to someone. But with the future in mind, let's explore at least four ways to profit from advertising. First, let's start with an important policy: Never rent, give, trade, or sell your e-mail names to anyone. Never. Period. And state this in your e-mail acquisition policy. In the offline world, renting a mailing list can be a juicy source of extra revenue. But online, the aversion to spam (unsolicited email) is so intense that you need to make a decision never to violate the goodwill of your "fish in training." This doesn't mean that you can't include a paid ad or two in your periodic newsletter.

Four Ways to Generate Advertising Revenues 1. Selling, renting, or trading banner ads on your Web site. 2. Selling, renting, or trading classified ad space on your Web site. 3. Selling, renting, or trading links from your site to another site. 4. Selling, renting, or trading advertising messages in your periodic e-zines. We explore exactly how to set up these advertising relationships in Chapter 13. Profit Center 5: Selling Picks and Shovels The fifth major way (there are dozens of minor ways) to earn income from your site is to profit from other people who are coming online. It has been widely reported that the only people who made any lasting money in the California and Alaska gold rushes were the people who supplied the picks and shovels and auxiliary services to the miners themselves. Surviving to this day is one of the most famous "pick-and-shovel coups," Levi's jeans. As an addendum to the Levi Strauss story from earlier in this book, it's instructive to note that Levi's are the only type of clothing created in the nineteenth century that is still being worn today. (I have several pairs hanging in my closet. Don't you?) Hundreds of millions of new Netpreneurs will join the online gold rush in the next decade. As in previous gold rushes, the majority will be disappointed in their prospecting. Not because there isn't gold in them thar hills but because these prospectors simply don't know how to go about finding it. That's where you come in. You can provide the picks and shovels for them. What are the picks and shovels of the Internet? 1. Web-hosting services 2. Web site design and consultation 3. Marketing advice 4. Traffic 5. Education and training 6. Advertising services 7. Affiliate programs to help new businesses get started 8. Computer hardware 9. Computer software 10. Credit card services

And many more. Just think of the kind of products, services, and information that it took and continues to take for you to get up to speed in your online business. You can provide the products, services, and answers to hundreds if not thousands of prospective miners. Why not profit from your education in the school of hard knocks? Read more on this in Chapter 14. Profit Center 6: Establishing Your Own Auction Have you ever bought something at an auction? What is there about auctions that is so seductive? Answer: It is a perfect formula for creating a feeding frenzy! Popularity + scarcity + urgency + curiosity = feeding frenzy The auction model applied to the Internet is one of those rare business ideas that looks, in retrospect, to be a stroke of pure genius: When millions of people focus on a single item for a limited time frame, those who wouldn't even consider buying such an item in an ordinary department store fight with total strangers to outbid each other over the Internet. Why shouldn't you participate? Don't you have some stuff in your possession or in your business inventory that would be perfect for an auction? Here are the three major benefits of setting up your own auction: 1. It can generate extra income for you. 2. It's a great way to advertise your Web site and expose more people to your ongoing business. 3. It's the hip thing to do.

CHAPTER EIGHT

BEYOND STICKINESS

You have three seconds. Snap. Snap. Snap. And they're gone. How can you get your visitors to linger longer? The technical Internet word for enticing surfers to hang around your Web page is stickiness. Stickiness is usually associated with three factors: 1. Duration: How long do your visitors spend at your site? 2. Depth: How deep will they go exploring? 3. Frequency: How often do your visitors return?

Big companies spend millions of dollars trying to increase the stickiness of their sites. Every month, Internet tracking company Media Metrics produces fancy statistics to show which sites won the battle of stickiness. The information is free and available at www.mediametrics.com. (Another great site for Internet statistics is www.forrester.com. Especially interesting is its list of the top e-commerce sites called the PowerRankings™.) Study the sample chart shown in Figure 8.1. In the month shown (August 2000), the average bingo player at bingo.com spent over 500 minutes (that's over eight hours!) playing bingo. The site passed all three tests for stickiness: duration, depth, and frequency. The reason the monster Internet sites like Yahoo!, eBay, and CNN are so interested in stickiness is that their primary model for making money is to sell advertising. They want to show advertisers how many sticky eyeballs are roaming around their site. These advertisers know that the longer those eyeballs ogle the pages, the greater the chance of someone clicking on their banner ads. That's why the monster Web sites are all hot and bothered about increasing their stickiness. In roaming around one of the stickiest sites, eBay, I stumbled across this quote about stickiness: But what exactly makes a site sticky? Doug McFarland, Senior Vice President and General Manager of Media Metrix explains that those mastering stickiness, offer a "mix of the four C's: community, content, communication and commerce." And of the mix, content appears to be the most important factor. Forrester Research's Media Field Study for January 1999 reveals 75% of users return to their favorite sites for the strong content and a regular churn of information. This sounds reasonable, but don't get too stuck on all of this talk about stickiness. If you're just launching a Web page, you won't be able to sell advertising space until your Web site has tens of thousands of hits per month. Your primary goal is not advertising. It's to be able to produce immediate (if not sooner) cash flow from the sale of products and services. You don't have the time or the money to develop a sticky site. Therefore, you're not so concerned with stickiness—how long your visitors stay, how deep they go, and how many times they come back. You are primarily concerned with quickness—the speed at which people agree to give you their e-mail addresses. If they'll give you permission to communicate with them, then you are in control of the stickiness! You have all the time in the world to educate them via e-mail about the wonders of your site. If you don't get that e-mail address—poof! They're gone. Stickiness is for big companies. Don't try to be the big guns. Their model is to cast a wide net and invite millions of people to stick to them. Their information is an inch deep and a mile wide. You can't compete with that. You have to do just the opposite: Your information or products should be an inch wide and a mile deep. Become an expert on a very narrow topic. You don't need millions of visitors to make your millions. Of the hundreds of millions of people on the Net, you need to convince only 10,000 highly targeted people to give you permission to develop a relationship with them. Those 10,000 people will make you rich. Why? Because 70 percent of those who use the Internet do so primarily to access their e-mail, not to surf. If you can get permission to send email messages to them, they may never again need to visit your site. It's not about getting their eyeballs to travel to your site. It's about getting their eyeballs focused on your e-mail messages. Those are the kinds of eyeballs you want! Ultimate Advantages of the Internet In reality, the concept of stickiness actually runs counter to the advantages of the Internet. When you think of the Internet, don't you think of speed? What people really want from the Internet is fast solutions to their problems. Do you really want the kind of customer who looks forward to spending several hours a week playing bingo online? (Get a life!) The kind of customers you're looking for don't want a sticky experience. They want fast results, immediate delivery, and instant gratification, mixed with some one-on-one interactivity. Fast. Free. Frequent. Hot tips. If you build your business around these advantages, you'll have all the business that you can handle.

"Quick"-iness versus Stickiness Eventually, you will seek to add stickiness to your site. But at first you're most concerned with "quick"-iness, the speed at which people agree to give you their e-mail addresses. Here are nine ways to improve the "quick"-iness and the stickiness of your site. Become an Expert on Instant Gratification In all of your marketing you should offer people an ethical bribe (a special report or some other goodie) to persuade them to take a peek at your site. When people hit your site, you only have three to five seconds to get them to stick. So you'd better make sure that the promised "free bonus" is immediately accessible. Spend a few short, enticing sentences reselling them on the value of your free gift. The more they sense the value of the gift you are offering them, the more you tap into the power of reciprocity. They feel they owe you a

few extra seconds to repay you for your generosity. Nothing wrong with that. We're all used to it. In fact, most of us sit through commercials to repay the broadcaster for providing such wonderful free TV programming. Remember, your first and most important task is to entice your visitors to leave their e-mail address and give you permission to contact them again. The more valuable your free gift, the less resistant they will be to leaving their e-mail address. Designing Your Irresistible Bundle of Goodies Everything on your site should point toward the bundle of goodies your visitors receive for leaving their e-mail address and their permission to let you contact them again. When these maybes leave their e-mail address, you begin to stock your Maybe Lake. It is critical to the long-term survival of your online business. In order to entice them to leave their e-mail address you must design a "welcome" basket filled with all kinds of wonderful free goodies. They should feel that they are completely crazy not to take advantage of your generosity. You want to access their greed button. Here are a few things you could offer your visitors for the privilege of giving you permission to prove what a peach of a person you are: Welcome Basket of Goodies • Free newsletter • Free special reports • Free book • Free coupons

• Free access to private information vault • Free checklists • Free quotes • Free samples • Free access to past newsletters • Free links to other great sites • Anything else you can think of Your goal is to instantly gratify your guests. If they sign up for your newsletter, send them an instant e-mail by autoresponder confirming their brilliant decision. Then reward them again! Give them another free gift. If they purchase a product, instantly surprise them with a first-timecustomer gift. When they receive their product, reward them again for their wise decision. Keep rewarding them for investing their precious time with you. This generosity will pay huge dividends. Transform Your Site into a Treasure Trove Visitors to your site should feel as though they just

stumbled onto Ali Baba's cave of treasures. "Open, Sesame," and the cave opens. They are free to pick through the jewels of wisdom that you have assembled there for them. From the first day you launch your site, you should be on the lookout for relevant chunks of information that you can load onto your site for the benefit of your visitors. Most of your visitors are in a Yellow Pages kind of searching mood, so your information will be welcomed. Give your visitors a good reason to add your site to their "favorites" list— and to tell others about their good fortune in finding you. If you are stingy with your free information, your visitors will be stingy with their pocketbooks and their recommendations. Fresh and Deep There are two kinds of information that your visitors will seek: (1) fresh, new, hot information—to keep them coming back for more—and (2) indepth, timeless information. The more you offer of both, the stickier your site will become. Give Your Visitors a Rich Experience Once you know that your marketing is working and that you are able to attract a steady stream of visitors and are gradually stocking your Maybe Lake, then you can add some extra features to your site.

Quote of the day. People love quotes. A new quote of the day would be very easy to program into your site. The wisdom of the ages can lend credibility to your offerings. Joke/cartoon of the day. Everyone loves a good laugh. With a little research you should be able to gather an archive of good, clean humor to fit into the overall theme of your business. Hall of fame for success stories. People love to see their name in lights. Actively gather success stories of people benefiting from your products and services. It not only builds credibility, it gives your customers an excuse to send other people to your site. Make a big deal of your satisfied customers and they will make a big deal of you.

Merchant implementation is easy. The ClickRewards account team helps market, promote and manage the rewards program, making it the easiest, most cost-effective relationship marketing tool available online. Your growing business may not yet be large enough to take advantage of such a program, but you should at least model what they're doing. It's obviously working. Reduce the Distance between Your Visitors and a Live Person The more and the faster your visitors can interact with real people, the stickier and "quickier" your site will become. This plays to the strengths of the Internet—speed and interactivity. If you can connect with your customers during their feeding frenzy, the more likely you are to make the sale. Unfortunately, this may go against the nature of the ideal hands-off, money-while-you-sleep kind of business that you'd like to create. As you design your business, you'll have to balance these two competing demands. Do you want to make money fast? Or do you want to make money without hassle? I'll bet you answered both, didn't you? Get People Together and They'll Reward You for It As your site grows, you will attract like-minded people; by default, you can become the central meeting point of a virtual community. Arthur Armstrong, author of Net Gain, has this to say: Virtual communities are groups of people who share common interests and needs who come together on-line. Most are drawn by the opportunity to share a sense of community with like-minded people—regardless of where they live. But virtual communities are more than just a social phenomena: what starts off being a group drawn together by common interests ends up being a group with a critical mass of purchasing power—based in part on the fact that in communities, members can exchange information with each other on such things as a product's price and quality. One of the leaders in creating the software for running virtual communities is InfoPop, found on the Net at www.infopop.com. You can actually download and test a working version of its product for free. It's called the Ultimate Bulletin Board. InfoPop's Web site describes some of the advan-tages of installing a bulletin board on your site.*

If done properly, it can be a win-win situation for everyone. For Consumers • Introduces others like themselves • Creates an instantly accessible marketplace • Fosters an open user forum and knowledge base • Reinforces purchase decisions • Concentrates group buying power—auctions, surplus • Answers service and support questions • Overcomes buyer objections • Shares product-usage tips For Sponsors and Marketers • Grants insights into buying public • Concentrates economic focus—auctions, surplus • Rapidly expands user base through "word-of-mouse" • Heightens brand awareness • Generates offer strategies and value propositions • Pretests new product development • Assembles an instant focus group • Generates content • Builds more meaningful service relationships • Engenders user-to-user product support Gateway to the Next Generation of Marketing • The ultimate realization of target marketing " Forms in stand market of your affinity group • Gains more personal information • Tests ideas and creates a value proposition • Lets your customers create your advertising • Relationship marketing, pure and simple • No postage stamps • No lost mail • No spam!

Community—The Key to Web Prosperity • Message board to attract and retain community • Visitors free to express themselves • Collaborative conversations over time • Greater Web site stickiness (duration of stay) • An essential forum for user communication There's a downside to building a virtual community: If your service isn't up to par, there is a forum for your customers to complain to each other and spread the word even faster. Before you build your community you'd better make sure that you build up your customer service. Now we've come to the final item on our stickiness/quickiness checklist. I've placed it last because its nature is fundamentally different from the others. The first eight points have to do with making your site addictive—creating reasons for people to buy now and in the future, again and again. The final item has to do with *making your site contagious—creating a buzz that spreads like wildfire. Study the Laws of Epidemics and the Principles of Contagiousness How can you create an explosion of traffic at your site? No amount of advertising can create word-of-mouse power. But you can help it get started. The Internet term for this phenomenon is viral marketing. The term was actually coined by the venture capital firm of Draper Fisher Jurvetson to describe the phenomenon of a company it funded in 1996 called Hotmail. Aside from having a great name, Hotmail was hot because of the way it was marketed. It spread like a virus, going from zero customers to over 40 million in only three years, increasing its subscriber base more rapidly than any company in the history of the world. As Business Week reported, the idea for Hotmail came about as almost an afterthought: The two principals, Sabeer Bhatia and Jack Smith . . . went to see Draper Fisher furvetson, but the investor was unimpressed by their idea for database software for the Net. As they were packing up to leave, [the venture capitalists] asked: "Do you have any other ideas?" Sabeer said they'd noodled over a scheme to offer free, advertising-supported E-mail over the Web. A week and a half later, the venture capitalists ponied up $300,000, and Hotmail was born.**

The key to Hotmail's phenomenal growth was the free price tag and the fact that every e-mail contained the following tag line and an implied endorsement by the sender: Get Your Private, Free Email at http://www.hotmail.com The more the service was used, the faster the word was spread. In 1998, Hotmail was sold to Microsoft for $400 million! Not a bad return for a free product. That is the payoff for having the most successful virally marketed business idea in history. Here is a list of a few other hot ideas that spread like wildfire: Harry Potter Hugely popular fantasy-novel series EBay World's leading online auction site Who Wants to Be a Millionaire? Hot ABC game show Survivor Hot CBS reality show Napster Hot free music site Surprise.com Hot gift *site BlueMountain.com Popular site for electronic greeting cards ICQ Instant messaging technology that signed up 12 million people before selling out to AOL for $300 million Amazon.com Signed up over 200,000 Netwide affiliates to spread its services The Blair Witch Project Popular movie, shot on shoestring, that grossed over $ 150 million All of these ideas spread through the population like a virus. How can you launch a virus? All you need is one good idea, right? And you need to understand the theory of a positive virus—how it spreads and what you can do to launch one of your own. There are four excellent books on the subject, all of which you should probably read if you really want to understand viral marketing. Luckily, you can download many excellent parts of them from the Internet for free. Permission Marketing (Seth Godin) www.permission.com The Tipping Point (Malcolm Gladwell) www.malcolmgladwell.com Unleasing the IdeaVirus (Seth Godin) www.ideavirus.com Anatomy of a Buzz (Emanuel Rosen) www.emanuel-rosen.com*

Start by going online and downloading your own copy of Godin's IdeaVirus book at www.ideavirus.com. Then download four free chapters of his first book, Permission Marketing. Good stuff. These books are more theoretical than practical—instructing us on the power of creating a buzz and hyping a product until it catches fire. Studying theory and case studies encourages you to come up with ways to create a positive epidemic of your ideas and products. There is a science to creating a buzz, especially if you know the parameters of the disease. Steve Jurvetson, the man who coined the term viral marketing, said this in a November 1998 article in Business 2.0: A good virus will look for prolific hosts (such as students) and tie itself to their high-frequency social interactions. Viral marketing is strongest when it taps into the breadth of its customers' weak connections to others. Tapping a customer's entire address book is more valuable than just reaching his or her best friend. The typical viral entry strategy is twofold: Minimize the friction of market entry and proliferation, and build in hooks to create barriers to switching. On his Web site, MalcolmGladwell.com, the author of The Tipping Point, says, Think, for a moment, about the concept of contagiousness. If I say that word to you, you think of colds and the flu or perhaps something very dangerous like HIV or Ebola. We have, in our minds, a very specific, biological, notion of what contagiousness means. But if there can be epidemics of crime or epidemics of fashion, there must be all kinds of things just as contagious as viruses. . . . The second of the principles of epidemics—that little changes can somehow have big effects and vice versa—is a also a fairly radical notion. . . . To appreciate the power of epidemics, we have to prepare ourselves for the possibility that sometimes big changes follow from small events, and that sometimes these changes can happen very quickly. . . . One of the things I'd like to do is to show people how to start "positive" epidemics of their own. The virtue of an epidemic, after all, is that just a little input is enough to get it started, and it can spread very, very quickly. That makes it something of obvious and enormous interest to everyone from educators trying to reach students to businesses trying to spread the word about their product, or for that matter to anyone who's trying to create a change with limited resources. The book has a number of case studies of people who have successfully started epidemics—an advertising agency, for example, and a breast cancer activist. I think they are really fascinating. I also take a pressing social issue, teenage smoking, and break it down and analyze what an epidemic approach to solving that problem would look like. The point is that by the end of the book I think the reader will have a clear idea of what starting an epidemic actually takes. This is not an abstract, academic book. It's very practical. And it's very hopeful. It's brain software. As I've said, studying these books will give you the theory of how to spread your product like a virus. This gives you the framework to develop a mind-set about making your message contagious. Here is a list of questions (again, thanks to Seth Godin) that you should be asking yourself as your create your marketing plan. Eight Questions to Use as a Self-Diagnostic Test 1. What can we do to make our product more virusworthy? 2. How likely are powerful sneezers to adopt our virus? 3. Do we know who the sneezers are and how to contact them? 4. Have we figured out what we want our sneezers to say? How are we teaching them to say it? 5. Is it possible to include our viral elements in our product? 6. Have we chosen a hive that we're capable of dominating? 7. How smooth is the transfer of the ideavirus? 8. Have we built in multiple feedback loops so that we can alter the virus as it moves and grows? To build on the theory of viral marketing, in Chapter 111 show you a very practical way to create a buzz.

CHAPTER NINE

How Fast Can You Go from Zero to Cash?

Suppose I drop you in a strange city for a week. I give you a place to sleep, food, and a computer with access to the Internet. Suppose you must start from scratch without relying on any of your own existing Web sites or databases. You have no products to market, no information to sell, no services to pitch. I'm talking about starting from ground zero. Zero to cash. How soon could you be up and making money? Would you even know where to start? In previous chapters, we've discussed the marketing principles that form the foundation—the bedrock—upon which the edifice of your cashflow machine will be constructed. Most businesses fail because they do not build on such a bedrock. Just in case you've forgotten, here they are again: 1. Find a school of hungry fish. (Who is your target audience?) 2. Find out what they're biting on. (What do they really want?) 3. Supercharge your bait. (Use USP and the 12 principles of persua sion.) 4. Build a massive Maybe Lake. (Create a space to turn strangers into friends.) 5. Catch and release. (Create a lifetime relationship with your clients.) Okay, Bob. Thanks for the refresher course. Time's running out! Now what? First, the zero to-cash scenario is obviously not a

normal situation. Most people who have time to launch a business will go through all of the steps I've outlined in this book: Research a group of hungry fish, figure out a product to satisfy their needs, create some bait, and start filling up their Maybe Lake. Several weeks or months later, they can start a fullblown marketing program. This, of course, is the prudent course. But for the sake of argument we're going to shorten the time frame to 72 hours. How fast can we have a Web site up and running? Of the dozens of places on the Net that will host your Web site for free, one company stands out for the depth and breadth of its services. You can be running your own e-business in minutes. Enough theory. Nobody learns to drive a car by reading about it. You have to get behind the wheel and do it. Let's go online. Right now. Stop reading and go fire up your computer. I'm assuming you have access to the Internet. Go there and get ready. Even if you already have your own Web site, let's go back to square one. I want to take you to a practice site . . . all ready for you to tinker. And the price is right. It's free. Go to www.vstore.com. This is a very neat site. You can literally design your own Web page from scratch. You don't have to be a genius to do it. And within minutes your store is stocked with as many as 1 million products—ready to sell, with a credit card merchant account already approved. You can literally be in business overnight. No kidding! The hard part is not setting up the store. It's getting people to visit that store. In this chapter, I show you rapid-fire techniques for filling up your new store with customers. But first, read what the company has to say about it.

CHAPTER TEN

Joint Ventures: High Leverage Ways to Make a Fortune Online

In an October 1996 issue of Fast Company, William C. Taylor interviewed Jeff Bezos, founder and CEO of Amazon.com. At the time of the interview, Amazon.com was barely a year old. I know you've heard the story a thousand times. But read it one more time. And see if you can spot the reason that I want you to read it. Jeff Bezos was a Wall Street trader and programming star, a top executive at fast-growing D.E. Shaw & Co., when a startling statistic caught his eye: World Wide Web usage was growing at 2,300% per year. He remembers his immediate reaction: "Anything growing that fast is going to be ubiquitous very quickly. It was my wake-up call." That was the summer of 1994. Bezos, now 32, quit D.E. Shaw and began methodically analyzing the most promising opportunities for Internet commerce. He concluded that online retailing was the next big thing, and that selling books over the Web was the first big retail opportunity. He moved to Seattle, raised several million dollars from private investors, and created the world's largest online bookstore. Amazon.com opened for business

in July 1995. It has since become one of the most admired and talked-about companies on the Web. . . . "In the summer of 1994, when the Web first caught my attention, I made a list of 20 product categories—books, music, computer hardware and software—and investigated the merits of selling them online. Books were far and away the best category. . . . There are so many of them! There are 1.5 million English-language books in print, 3 million books in all languages worldwide. This volume defined the opportunity. . . . But the largest physical bookstore in the world has only 175,000 titles. We have 1.1 million titles. There's no way you can build a store to handle 1.1 million titles. And you can't offer our selection in a catalog. If you printed the Amazon.com catalog, it would be the size of seven New York City phone books. The only way to build a 1.1 million-title bookstore is on the Web. . . . It sounds counterintuitive, but physical location is very important for the success of a virtual business. We could have started Amazon.com anywhere. We chose Seattle because it met a rigorous set of criteria. It had to be a place with lots of technical talent. It had to be near a place with large numbers of books. It had to be a nice place to live—great people won't work in places they don't want to live. Finally, it had to be in a small state. In the mail-order business, you have to charge sales tax to customers who live in any state where you have a business presence. It made no sense for us to be in California or New York. Obviously Seattle has a great programming culture. And it's close to Roseburg, Oregon, which has one of the biggest book warehouses in the world. We thought about the Bay Area, which is the single best source for technical talent. But it didn't pass the small-state test. I even investigated whether we could set up Amazon.com on an Indian reservation near San Francisco. This way we could have access to talent without all the tax consequences. Unfortunately, the government thought of that first." Did you get it? If you didn't, go back and read it again. Jeff Bezos saw an idea, acted on his hunch, quit his job, moved across the country, and did whatever it took to turn his idea into reality. His reward was fame and fortune. Now I'm going to share with you the highest-probability method for you to do the same thing—perhaps minus the fame. On second thought, who am I to limit your dreams? Go for it. It's probably too late to go head-to-head with the likes of Amazon. Your vein of gold is more likely to come by picking a very narrow sliver of the pie and dominating it. I'll assume that you have decided on your unique idea, identified your target audience, decided on your USP, and lined up your products. Now what? In the previous chapters, you've learned at least six major ways to drive traffic to your site so visitors can buy your products. How would you like to learn a powerful, high-speed shortcut to doubling, tripling, even quadrupling your sales online? Let me introduce you to your online mentor for this chapter. His name is Mike Enlow. Ever heard of him? He shows you how to start with nothing and make a fortune. He shows you how to use a powerful form of leverage available to any beginner. What is that leverage? It is the power of the existing relationship that other businesses have with their current customers. In other words, you don't have to launch your brand-new business into the cold, cold world. You can gain immediate access to customers through the back door—a sort of Trojan horse strategy. You can go from the back of the line to the front of the line. The velvet rope will no longer keep you out. I have specifically chosen Mike Enlow to share this strategy with you because, once you hear his story, you realize that you have no excuses. If Mike can make it, so can you. Mike describes himself as "a Mississippi backwoods country boy, without even a high school diploma." In 1983, while he was working in Louisiana, his life changed forever. Here is Mike's story in his own words. It was August 28, 1983, 4:50 P.M. I was on my Yamaha 400, burning up the back roads. I was heading home to get ready for a singing engagement when I rounded a curve and met a pickup truck heading straight for me in my lane. We hit head-on. Then I died. I was out of my body for a time. I saw the ambulance arrive; 1 saw the girl who was driving the pickup crying beside my body; and I heard everything the paramedics said as they began to revive me. Just as I was starting to realize I didn't want to return, I was flooded with excruciating pain as I rushed back into my body, which was smashed to pieces. The agony I felt was indescribable. I was barely conscious but I remember telling the girl driving the truck not to cry. I was rushed to the emergency room and my family was notified. Laura, my wife, and I were separated at this time, and she was out of town. I lay there and cried for my mother to bring me some Chap Stick because my lips were dry and burning badly. The pain had escalated from indescribable to unbearable by this time. My brother was there beside me in the ER, and when he asked me what he could do for me, I asked him to let me bite his finger to ease the pain. I had emergency surgery to insert six steel rods in my legs. I had neck and back fractures; my helmet had cracked, and I had a concussion, abrasions, broken ribs, and my arm was crushed. On the whole, it just wasn't a real good day. The doctors told me I was in critical condition. No one could tell me whether I'd walk again or be more than minimally functional. I spent weeks in the hospital, fighting the pain and holding on to my will to survive. I asked one of the doctors if I'd ever be able to play my guitar again. He said no. So I asked a friend to bring my guitar to the hospital. He placed it in my hands, and it hurt like nobody's business, but with a roomful of nurses I played that guitar until they cried. One small victory already. I knew then that I was going to make it out of there. I think they did, too. In all, I had seven surgeries. I'd suffered compression fractures, and the doctors warned me I might never be able to work again. I finally made it out of the hospital, confined to a wheelchair but determined to survive somehow. When I got home, I had a four-year-old daughter to care for, with no one there to care for me. I had no insurance, no income, no savings—absolutely nothing. Eventually the bank came and took everything. My car, my furniture, everything I had. I was left with nothing and totally helpless. My landlord was sympathetic and let me stay in the house I was living in. Luckily, two neighbors who lived on either side of me brought my daughter and me food every day. I found out later that these people hated each other, but each brought us food every day, not knowing the other was doing it, too. Strangely enough, they never once showed up at the same time. I survived, and eight months later I moved back to Mississippi. I began to reestablish my income by selling specialty ads while still in the wheelchair, literally wheeling myself from door to door, often asking strangers on the street to lift me up the stairs. It took me two years to get out of that wheelchair. I'll never forget the day I stood up, pushed the chair back, and walked away from it. I still keep that wheelchair, just to remind me of what I nearly lost, all that I gained, and all that I conquered. If I walked away from that chair, there's nothing I can't do. Eighteen years later, Mike Enlow has become one of the top marketing gurus in the world. His businesses have grossed millions of dollars, and his programs have helped thousands raise themselves, as their mentor did, from nothing to levels of success only imagined by most people. Mike still suffers chronic pain from his motorcycle accident, but he thanks God for every extra day he's been given to spread his positive message. I asked Mike to share with you the number one secret of his success. Read very carefully, because these ideas have generated hundreds of millions of dollars' worth of business for Mike and his students. Mike's formula was perfected in the early 1990s, when the Internet was just a gleam in Jeff Bezos's eye. I personally agree with Mike that this secret will be your fastest route to online success in marketing your product. Here is the formula in Mike Enlow's own words.

How to Create Wealth from Others' Overlooked Assets

Few believe me when I tell them of the fortunes they can make starting with nothing. Sometimes I feel as though I'm the only one with macroscopic glasses (to see the big picture) when examining businesses and the many opportunities for creating additional cash flow. Nearly every business I consult with has no less than 3 (and often 10) different ways to almost immediately create additional cash flow from its existing efforts, clients, and advertisements. I'm going to share with you one of the simplest of these concepts, which I call joint venture alliances or co-ventures. I assume you have no knowledge of marketing for the benefit of those of you who are unfamiliar with my marketing techniques. Let's begin. Joint Venture Alliances I've discovered many working marketing concepts and systems. All of them are centered around one word: leverage! I want to show you how to use leverage to get greater profits and greater satisfaction out of every dollar spent and every effort expended. Over the years, I've learned that every business has one need in common—the need to create more cash flow than is spent on overhead. Tens of thousands of businesses do this very successfully. Unfortunately, they overlook many opportunities to gain greater leverage and reap greater rewards from what they do. It takes just as much energy to create an advertisement that produces 100 sales (or leads) as it does to produce 1,000. In the next few pages I'm going to teach you one of the fastest and easiest ways for any business owner to increase his or her profits by as much as 300 percent and do so with nobility. One of the most ridiculous mistakes and oversights in marketing is the failure to recognize the true value of the relationship a business owner has with his or her customers, vendors, and others with whom they deal on a daily basis. Properly utilizing this overlooked asset can mean thousands, and often tens of thousands, of dollars in increased revenue and goodwill. Let me explain. People making a purchase prefer to buy from someone they trust and who has treated them fairly in the past. If you were to rent a cold list (a list of names of people who know nothing about me, my company, product, service, or offer) you might, with a well-crafted sales letter or presentation, get a 1 to 3 percent response rate on the offer. However, if you go to the owner of that same list and structure a deal where the owner writes or presents the very same offer to the very same people, you will see a response rate that is so much higher it boggles the mind. I've seen response rates to this type of offer (call it an endorsed offer) that skyrocket to as high as 33 percent! This is an increase in response rate of between 1,100 to 3,300 percent! Accordingly, you can literally earn a fortune by showing others how to use this principle to create win-win deals. A good example of using this concept happened a few Christmases ago with a client of mine who is in the pharmacy business. My client had approximately 10,000 customers on file, all of whom loved and trusted him for the excellent service they had received over the years. However, I discovered my client had never ever used this incredible asset of trust in a noble win-win deal. Like too many businesspeople, my client was myopic (unable to see the big picture) in observing his own business. He failed to realize that although his business is selling pharmaceutical products and supplies, all his customers purchase many other products and services (dry cleaning, groceries, cars, insurance, accounting services, etc.). The relationship with customers provides business owners with the incredible opportunity to use the endorsed offer. By doing a joint venture, whereby they recommend or refer their customers to another professional and noble company, they could share in a percentage of the profits from the newfound business they create for the company they endorse. In this particular situation, I learned that my client was friendly with a jeweler in town, and Christmas was rapidly approaching. I saw an instant jackpot. (By the way, these deals can be created without a prior relationship with the vendor you will endorse.) Here's a brief overview of what can happen with joint ventures, or endorsed offers. I immediately contacted and interviewed the jeweler to get the "golden nuggets" needed to create a letter for my pharmacy client to share with his customers. I learned that this jeweler regularly flew to New York to purchase diamonds, emeralds, rubies, and other precious stones. More important, by teaming up with another jeweler in New Orleans, this jeweler literally saved a fortune by buying in bulk.

Dear Customers and Friends, Last week my wife and I were browsing through the many Christmas card binders to select a suitable Christmas card to mail to you, our customers, to express our appreciation for your patronage. Of the many hundreds of Christmas cards available, we couldn't find a single card that expressed our heartfelt feelings and appreciation to our cus-tomers. After all, it is customers like you who helped us to send our two children to college and build our business to be one of the most successful pharmacies in the city. Frankly, I decided to say thank-you in a very special way—with actions, not words. Let me explain. One of my dearest friends, a local jeweler, has the largest selection of diamonds, rubies, emeralds, watches, and other inventory in the area, but more important, he has developed an incredible method of wholesale purchasing that allows him to save a fortune. As we were talking, I explained how I wanted to do something very special for my friends and customers this Christmas to express my gratitude for their business. I further explained how I wanted to do something that would benefit and thank them with actions rather than just words in a Christmas card. After a bit of arm-twisting, my jeweler friend agreed to offer a 20 percent discount to my customers who show this letter during their holiday shopping! This discount applies to any purchase you make in his store this year. This is my special way of saying thank-you to my valued customers. And my jeweler friend, who offers only the finest-quality jewelry, agreed to participate because he believes you will continue to be his customer for years to come. So feel free to take this letter to XYZ Jewelers anytime between now and Christmas and you will receive a privileged discount of 20 percent off any purchases—as *well as VIP treatment from my friend. Since almost everyone buys jewelry during the Christmas season, my wife and I feel this is a much better way of saying thank-you than any card we could send. Enjoy, and Merry Christmas, > Don and Susan Smith, XYZ Pharmacy RS. Oh yes, he did request that I ask you to slide this letter to him inconspicuously so that his other customers won't feel slighted. They aren't getting this VIP discount. Please do me this kind favor when you go in. This letter of endorsement became the pharmacy's Christmas card for that year. We had prearranged a special deal whereby XYZ Pharmacy would receive half of the profits generated by the letter. Because of that, we earned an incredible $87,550 mailing Christmas cards instead of incurring a $5,000 cost to mail the usual Christmas cards to 10,000 people.*

The jeweler was delighted after he'd been briefed about how a certain percentage of these newfound customers would become lifelong customers. This marketing education is the key to getting the most from deals like this. Let me share the approach. First you have to understand that most people fail to realize the lifetime value of a customer. This is your opportunity to educate the joint venture associate you wish to approach. Few businesspeople realize the residual value of new customers. Not all customers will come back. This will be true even if you give them the best quality, pricing, and service. However, a certain percentage of them will come back. In this case, over 2,780 people took the pharmacist up on his offer. The jeweler gave away the lion's share of the front-end profit, but he will earn much more than most realize. Let's look at a hypothetical example. Assume only 10 percent of those who took advantage of the offer return the following year and make an average purchase of only $500. The jeweler not only profits from the initial deal, but he earns an additional $70,000 because of the pharmacist's referral. Jewelry is generally "keystone-priced"—meaning it sells at a 100 percent markup. If only 10 percent of the *people return and spend an average of $500, that brings in an additional $139,000. At keystone pricing, that's an additional $69,500 profit for the jeweler! This doesn't even take into account the fact that satisfied customers may return year after year, creating profits that may have been nonexistent without the endorsement of the pharmacist. Are you beginning to see the possibilities? They are astronomical!*

You can make deals like these with car dealers, contractors, dentists, restaurants—almost any kind of business you can imagine. The beauty of it is that this is a win-win deal for everyone, and you are paid for arranging the deals. In a moment, I'll show you how the endorsed-mailing approach works extremely well on the Internet. Other Approaches In the preceding example we used Christmas as a "reason why," but you can create a host of reasons for deals like these: • "We've just discovered the most incredible . . . " • "We've learned of a secret method . . ." • "Since my friend is just getting off the ground . . ." • "This is the most incredible way for you to . . ." • "It's only fair to tell you before the rest of the world learns that. . ." • "We felt we would be remiss if we didn't offer you the first opportunity to try . . . " The number of approaches is unlimited! I can't think of a single business that couldn't make more money by properly utilizing its customer base to endorse a quality product or service. How Do You Get These Deals! One of the most successful ways to get deals like these is to approach your target market with a pitch like this: "/// show you how to properly utilize an asset you are overlooking and make you look like the knight in shining armor, would you be willing to share 50 percent of the newfound profits with me?" There are no hard-and-fast rules. You should structure the deal in whatever way you must. The preceding suggestion has proven itself to be a great approach, especially when you guarantee to shoulder the cost to do the deal and take your profits only on the additional income you generate. Most will see the light after a few minutes. How Do You Ensure You Get Paid! I use a letter of nondisclosure, stipulating the basic terms of the arrangement, before I share the secret of this incredible concept. Again, the rules are not set in granite. You should be as flexible as you need to be to get the deal. It all depends on the size, volume, and type of deal and your level of involvement. However, you can earn a very respectable income by using this concept to show businesspeople how to redeploy their existing assets.

How Do You Get Started! Getting started is easy. All you have to do is identify the potential partners. Then write a letter similar to the one that follows. Also, be sure to follow up the letter with a phone call. Do not share the intellectual property you have to offer until you have your agreement signed by all parties who will be participating. The following door opener will have your phone ringing off the hook: Dear Store Owner: My name is [your name here]. I am a marketing consultant who specializes in creating immediate additional cash flow to you at literally no cost to you. Over the years I've developed a number of intellectual property concepts that have proven themselves to increase cash flow almost immediately by using little-known, overlooked techniques. People from almost every business and industry have used the concepts I want to share with you—with extraordinary success. I have already taken the liberty to look over your business and am certain I can create a surprisingly large amount of cash for you. I will do so on a strict contingency basis. In fact, since I have already found the perfect deal for you, I will put my money into the marketing of the concept. I will call you on Tuesday or Thursday to discuss this in greater detail. AJII ask is that you call my voice mail, state your company name, and specify the day that's best for you so we can get together and get the show on the road. I do these types of deals nationwide, so please call right away so I can fit you into my schedule on the days specified. I guarantee that you will be blown away and quite surprised by how this new concept can add to your bottom line in a matter of weeks. I do all the work, and you reap the benefits. Since I am very selective in choosing clients with whom to share this incredible concept, I must ask you to sign a simple letter of understanding before I can tell you the details of the deal I have in mind for you. Sincerely, Your Name Marketing Firm Name RS. If the dates I've specified are inconvenient for you, go ahead and call just to let me know you are interested. I'll try to arrange a time that is mutually convenient since the deal I have in mind for you is rather significant.

You can be assured that you will receive responses to this letter. Just set up your voice mail and be sure to find the matching product or service before you mail the letter. How Do I Know Which Products Will Work with Which Clients? Well, there are no set rules. With a little creative thought, you can come up with dozens of product ideas. Think of the example of the pharmacy and the jewelry store. What made this deal work? The pharmacy had a list of satisfied customers. The jewelry store had the ability to give a great deal. Both businesses won! As I said earlier, you need to educate one side regarding the lifetime value of gaining new customers in order to get the best deal. You can often get as much as 100 percent of the profit of the sales made by your endorser by simply explaining this misunderstood marketing principle. How Do I Get the Sweetest Deals! If I were starting from scratch I would seek out companies with products to sell as opposed to service businesses. These deals are the easiest to get. When you work with attorneys, accountants, and other service businesses, the money trickles in slowly. With product sales, the money comes in over a two- to three-week period. Look for companies that have an established customer database and, more important, have a good, strong relationship with their customers. The stronger the relationship, the stronger the endorsement. The stronger the endorsement, the greater the profits. Just look for situations in which the endorser has a lot of contact with customers. Preferably, endorsers should be in contact with their customers at least monthly. The world is a big ocean of products and services. You have to find only one or two products that will yield successful results to your clients. Not only does this provide you with immediate income, it also sets you up to effect similar deals with the same clients in the future. Here are a few examples of the kind of deals I would put together right away: Marry car dealers with detail shops that maintain the appearance of cars—and structure the deals so that the detail company offers longterm (one-year) contracts at a savings of X percentage. Introduce dental patients to companies who sell teeth whitener. Get them on a monthly purchase deal whereby their credit cards are automatically billed and the whitener is automatically shipped for as long as the customer wants the product.

Marry Internet service providers with schools that teach Internet classes. Then bring in software vendors to introduce their products to these students — for an extra profit center — including a percentage of the profits from students who upgrade the software in the long term. This is a trilateral joint venture. As you see, the profit potentials are endless! Arrange deals whereby software vendors share lists and make offers to one another's customer base. Of course, set it up to take your piece of the pie. . . . This is a very lucrative area, especially if you arrange the deal so that you continue to get a percentage of upgrades. I hope you are beginning to see the potential. I've used this single concept to earn millions of dollars. If I had to choose one single way to make money, this would be it. I'll never forget how I made this discovery. In the early 1 990s, I traveled extensively to study the greatest marketing minds on earth. I met and subsequently became very good friends with Gary Halbert, a highly astute marketing mind and writer of advertising sales copy (space ads, direct-mail sales letters, radio scripts, etc.). Gary taught me a lot about marketing, especially the power of endorsement mailings, the ultimate marketing method!

CHAPTER ELEVEN

AFFILIATE PROGRAMS: CASH IN BY SELLING OTHER PEOPLE'S STUFF

power of affiliate programs. In this chapter, I'm going to show you how. Just for fun, log on to the Internet and check out this site: www.associate-it.com (directory of Associate programs) This is one of the top sites tracking the hundreds of affiliate programs on the Net. There is something here for any taste or multiple tastes. But how do you make money from an affiliate program? I've asked my good friend, Bob Gatchel, owner of InternetCheapskate.com and author of The Cheapskate's Guide to Internet Marketing, to share some of his marketing insights. Whether you're a newbie to the Net or an established Internet business, you can learn from his "frugal" wisdom. If they'd listened to Bob, a lot of Internet start-ups would still be up and cranking instead of dead and dying. Bob and his wife Joyce have been instrumental in mentoring me in the exciting field of Internet marketing, so I know you are in good hands. Take it away, Bob. The Hidden Power of Affiliate Programs How would you like to start your own proven, online marketing business without having to spend tons of money—even without having a Web site? How would you like a business where you do not have to stock products, handle money, ship products, or deal with customer service issues—but you still make money with that product line? Can that really happen? Can this situation be true? Absolutely, by using the power of the Internet's best-kept secret, the affiliate program. Affiliate programs are probably the fastest, easiest, and most profitable way to make money on the Internet! An affiliate program is nothing more than a joint venture between someone like you, a marketer, and a company that wants to promote a product. Basically, the company with the product provides the product, the Web site, the customer service, the order handling, and the fulfillment. But the company also gives you a link so that when you refer clients to purchase its products, you earn a nice commission from every sale! The company wins because it has thousands of marketers all over the world recommending its products. You win by being paid to market top-notch products and services. Bottom line, you simply refer people to these sites and you're paid for any resulting sales—period! Some of the biggest companies in the world are using affiliate programs to expand their markets (Dell Computer, Sprint PCS, Staples, OfficeMax, L.L. Bean, and many, many others). And more companies are jumping onto the e-commerce/affiliate bandwagon every day. There are affiliate programs for food, clothing, software, computers, toys, electronics, longdistance service, and even medicine! You can literally build your own online store with tons of different products and receive commissions for simply referring people to buy from these sites! The benefits of using affiliate programs to make money on the Internet are quite obvious: 1. It is easy! You don't need to create a product or service. You never need to worry about spending the time and money to build and maintain a Web site. You never need to worry about customer service, shipping, or even getting a merchant account to accept credit cards. The company handles every one of those details.

2. You can make money fast. Since you need not be concerned with all of the technical details of a Web site and need not build your own company to handle order issues, you can start by simply concentrat ing on advertising your special link to these sites. You can literally begin making money almost immediately. In some cases, people have been getting their first orders within days . . . hours . . . or even minutes! 3. You can be sure that the products you are offering will sell! Suppose you take the time to build your own product, company, and Web site, and your product doesn't go over well. Then you are kind of stuck, since you spent so much time and effort to make a go of it. Being a pioneer and starting a new business can be tough. You end up with a lot of arrows in your back. In an affiliate program, you don't need to reinvent the wheel—the hard work has been done. The market research, product development, and online sales materials have been professionally created. You literally have hundreds of thousands of dollars of marketing and market research done for you. And it costs you nothing to use it! 4. You can run more than one program and create multiple streams of affiliate income. You are never locked into one product. You have as many or as few affiliate programs at your disposal as you wish. I recommend that you try to concentrate on just a few programs and work them well, but if you find that there is a new market to capture and money to be made with a new product, then just sign up for the program and start promoting! Affiliate programs allow you to be an online business change agent. 5. Free marketing training and tools are provided by the company. When you sign up for an affiliate program (which is normally free), you get not only the ability to represent that company's product line with no hassle to you, but many companies provide you, the marketer, with tons of great marketing training material. You often get sample advertising copy, sample banners to use on Web sites, and sample sales letters. Again, you are getting some of the best marketing tools and training available to help make YOU and the COM PANY successful—for FREE! So, where do you find these programs ? Affiliate programs are all over the Internet. If you visit almost any online e-commerce Web site or any site that sells products, you will often see a link to "Join the affiliate program" or "Earn cash" button. As you browse, be sure to look for affiliate opportunities from your favorite online stores.

Several great online databases not only list affiliate programs, but also rate them on how well they pay and how they rank against other affiliate programs..

If you go to any search engine and use the term "Affiliate program," you will find other resources. Remember, the Internet is in a constant state of change, and this list is just a start. Affiliate Programs: Make Money Now ... and More Money Later! As I have often taught my Internet marketing students, an affiliate program is a vital part of any online business venture. Even if you have a well-tested product or service, even if you have a productive and profitable Web site or online marketing presence, an affiliate program is a must to help generate another stream of cash and provide more service to your online customers. But there is another aspect to an affiliate program that is often overlooked—even by some of the best marketing minds in the world—and that is using affiliate programs to build a huge customer list. Too often, people think only about the immediate money that can be made from an affiliate program, and that is fine. You can, indeed, with good marketing and advertising, make a great income from an affiliate program. But many times people forget that these customers could actually be good future customers for other products. You see, every direct marketer or mail-order marketer knows the value of having a customer list. If you read any book on marketing, every single one talks about the list you should have. Well, Internet marketing is no different. Internet marketing is a direct extension of offline marketing, and the concepts of direct marketing and mail order apply equally as well here. Unfortunately, average folks use an affiliate program as follows: 1. They run an ad. 2. The ad contains their special affiliate link. 3. The customer goes to the site . . . and maybe buys. 4. The affiliate gets a commission if the sale is made.

Basically, such affiliates are doing what I call filter-feeder marketing. They just throw out the link to their affiliate program and hope for the best. Oftentimes, they do get the sales and make money. But this is a huge lack of potential. You see, many marketing gurus state that the secret to successful marketing is to follow up with prospects and remind them of the offer. In filter-feeder marketing there is no follow-up by the marketer. If they could somehow capture the leads before they send them on to the company affiliate site, then they could keep in touch with these prospects and help them make the decision to purchase. Therefore, the more advanced marketer will do this: 1. Run the ad. 2. Direct the prospect to contact the marketer (that's you). 3. The marketer captures the e-mail and name. 4. The marketer sends the prospect to the affiliate link. 5. The customer may or may not purchase anything. 6. The marketer follows up and continues to pitch the product. 7. More customers will buy. The fortune is in the follow-up! This is much better than filter-feeder marketing because it's been shown that the fortune is in the follow-up. From my own experience and the experiences of my students, following up with prospects causes the buy ratio to increase dramatically. The next problem occurs if you are victim of your own success. If you are getting tons of replies, you need to track when the lead came in, when you sent the first follow-up message, and when to send subsequent follow-ups. In our systems, we follow up anywhere from 7 to 10 times with a prospect. Could you imagine trying to keep track of which person gets what follow-up message and when? Believe me, if you try to do this manually, you can spend hours and hours each day, and it will drive you crazy. Even though you captured the leads, managing them can be a nightmare. The Optimal Solution Since the Internet is all about automation and using technology to make our lives simpler, we recommend a system that uses a specialized Internet marketing tool called a sequential or automatic follow-up autoresponder. Basically, it's a way to put all of your follow-up on autopilot. An autoresponder is nothing more than a little online robot that spits out predetermined messages to anyone who contacts it via e-mail. If you send an e-mail to this robot, it will send out your sales message, letter, or pitch 24 hours a day 7 days a week without fail. But these sequential or timed autoresponders go one better. In addition to sending out the first message for you, you can upload all sequential follow-up messages and have them e-mailed automatically to the appropriate prospect at the appropriate time—all without your intervention. A prospect could get your first sales letter right away, three days later get the next one, a day later get another one, five days later get the next, and so on. You program which message goes out when based on the prospect's initial contact with your little e-mail robot. This follow-up autoresponder literally puts your entire lead capture and follow-up management on autopilot!

As you can see, with no Web site, no product, no merchant account, and no delivery hassles, my investment of $34.50 yielded $55.50 in profit. But that is not the end of the story. . . . Reinvest and expand! I reinvested $55.50 by running ads in five e-zines at an average cost per ad of approximately $10.00. Average circulation was approximately 9,000. Same Program, Same Ads, Same System • Targeted to working moms • Used autoresponder system • Followed up for two weeks Responses • 42 total responses (about 0.05%) • Seven sales @ $30 = $210 Bottom Line Gross Sales $210 Expenses: Autoresponder ($27) E-zine advertisement ($0) (Remember, I reinvested the $55.50 I made last month, so *there was no out-of-pocket advertising cost this month!) Net profit $183 (with a lower response and conversion) After two months of this campaign we have generated the following: Total profits: $183.00 Total new leads: 57 This means I got paid $3.21 for every lead that I generated. Now this may not seem like a lot of money. But you can rest assured that I continued to reinvest in my system, expanding until I was getting tons of leads. Not all of my campaigns were successful; sometimes I actually had a cost per lead. However, overall I have never lost any money on creating my leads list.*

This means I got paid $3.21 for every lead that I generated. Now this may not seem like a lot of money. But you can rest assured that I continued to reinvest in my system, expanding until I was getting tons of leads. Not all of my campaigns were successful; sometimes I actually had a cost per lead. However, overall I have never lost any money on creating my leads list. Read that again: I have never lost money generating my leads with this system.

If you are a direct marketer, you fully understand the power of what I just said. In direct mail and mail order, you often have to spend money on leads—but using an affiliate program in this manner can act as a "selffunded proposal" and actually pay you money to generate leads. Even if I broke even and didn't make or lose one penny but generated hundreds of leads in the process, I would still be very successful. Why? Because I now have a free list of prospects to market to again and again . . . and again . . . via e mail. Do you think I stop promoting products to these leads when I get them? Do you think I just stop after I make a few bucks from this affiliate sale? No way! I found a comparable affiliate program with products and services that would appeal to the targeted list I created. Guess what I did? You are right! I e-mailed my prospects a few weeks later thanking them *for their interest in my previous offer and directing them to the other program I was offering. Many did indeed purchase those products, and yes, I made more money from those same leads. I discovered yet another way to make money with my database—I found other people on the Internet with whom to joint-venture and swap leads. If I had 1,000 leads who showed interest in my products in the past and my new partner had a comparable product, we agreed to an even exchange of leads and marketed our respective affiliate programs to those new people. I also sold my older leads lists to other marketers. That single $50 sale translated to many, many other streams of income. The moral of the story is, yes, use affiliate programs to make money, but the ultimate goal is to use them to create a targeted e-mail list that will help you build long-term, back-end, and follow-up sales in the future. I hope that this introduction gives you a different view on how to use affiliate programs to turbocharge your online marketing ventures. If you would like to reach me to discuss this and other marketing concepts, just visit my site at Best of success with your online marketing!**

One of the most popular affiliate programs on the Web was launched by Dr. Ken Evoy. Ken is president of SiteSell.com, whose 5 Pillar Program is considered by many experts to be the most innovative, partnership-oriented and productive affiliate program on the Net. Here is how he did it. Building a Powerful Affiliate Program in 10 Days or Less Being a great affiliate is not about selling. . . . It's about preselling. The goal of any business, including your affiliate business, is to maximize profits. Profit is simply your income minus your expenses. As an affiliate, there are exactly two ways to increase your income: 1. Refer more visitors to the merchants you represent. 2. Increase the conversion rate (i.e., the percent of your referrals who deliver the response for which your merchant pays, whether it be a sale or a lead). Simple, right? If you refer 100 visitors per day to a merchant, and 1 percent buy, you are paid for that one* *purchase. If you send 1,000 visitors per day, and 3 percent buy, you are paid for 30 purchases. Yes, 30 times more! So it's pretty clear how to maximize affiliate income! Of course, every business has expenses, too. Maximizing profits does not imply that you must minimize expenses. After all, if you spend no money or time on a business . . . you have no business! You must get the best possible traffic-building and sales-converting results for every dollar you spend . . . and for every hour you spend on your business. Let's examine expenses by asking two questions.*

Let's break that down. For your affiliate Web site to generate traffic to your merchants, it must do the following two things well: 1. Rank well at the search engines so that it pulls in lots of traffic. So far, though, that traffic is still on your site. Therefore, it's not generating income yet. Your visitors are just looking around. So you must. . . 2. Get those visitors to click through to your merchants. (Some affiliate program models can actually place merchant offerings on your Web site. In this case, your traffic does not actually visit your merchant's site. But you still have to get the click to generate income.) Question 2: What does it cost to maximize conversion rates? Good news! Maximizing your conversion rate (CR) is simply a question of doing things right. There is no extra dollar or time cost to boosting conversion rates at your merchants' sites. Your goals, and your only goals, are as follows: 1. Maximize traffic to your merchants, spending only dollars and time that maximize profits. 2. Maximize conversion rates. Do things right (no expense).

grow geometrically when you concentrate on maximizing both traffic and conversion rates. I have spent quite a bit of time reviewing the results of affiliates to my own affiliate program (5 Pillar Program). Here is what I've discovered: The number one reason for low traffic and terrible conversion rates is banner ads! Retinal studies have shown that Web surfers actually avoid banners. Yes, their eyes look away! Click-throughs have plummeted to under onehalf of 1 percent. For the few who do click, my research shows that banners are worse than futile—they are counterproductive. My 5 Pillar Program affiliates who rely on banners have an average conversion rate of 0.5 percent. But those who use in-context text links (text links that are part of the content of the Web page) average over 3.5 percent! How's that for a reason not to use banners? Why does this happen? Banners are cheesy and hurt your credibility because visitors arrive feeling used rather than informed. They arrive in a resistant mind-set rather than with an open, ready-to-buy attitude. Conclusion? Don't use banners. Yes, I know, they're so-o-o-o-o easy. It's always easy not to make money. That's how all those get-rich-quick schemers do so well . . . the allure of easy money. No such thing. If you simply must use banners, save them for products that you don't really feel great about recommending. (That way, you don't hurt your credibility—after all, it's only advertising.) Save your in-context text links for super companies with wonderful products that deliver true value to your reader. Beside the obvious futility of banners, I've spotted another major error: selling instead of presetting. Picture this: A visitor arrives at an affiliate's site that is really just one, big sales site. Put yourself in these visitors' shoes for a moment. They don't see inspiring, editorial content—they see a sales effort. But they were searching for content! People resist sales efforts, so your click-through rate actually goes down. Result? Poor conversion rate. If your site is basically a bunch of sales letters, you have not yet built your credibility and likability with this visitor. Your visitors end up feeling "pitched to." And then they feel "double-pitched" if they click through to your merchant's site. That's why the conversion rate (CR) actually goes down. To make things worse, as they smell a sales pitch, your visitors become less likely to click! So referred traffic drops, too. (As a point of interest, women now represent 50 percent of all surfers, and they control approximately 80 percent of all shopping dollars.)

Let's see. . . . Referred traffic is down. Conversion rate is down. We're going in the wrong direction! Conclusion? Don't sell! Instead, warm up your visitors by presetting them with great content that they value and respect. They'll click through with pleasure, arriving at your merchants' sites in an open-to-buy mind-set. It's your presell effort that will boost your traffic to merchants and your conversion rate, which in turn maximizes your income. Put yourself in your customers' shoes. What will they think, how will they feel as visitors to your site? Consider how much higher your CR would be if visitors found you in a bona fide manner (e.g., as a result of using a search engine), then became friends (or trusting admirers if you do a truly awesome job!) because you provided excellent content that eventually led to a context-appropriate recommendation. Preselling is really all about selling yourself to your customer every step of the way. You reach the right folks in a proper fashion; you deliver valuable, appropriate editorial content; and you recommend visitors to your merchant after they have come to respect and like you. Your CR will soar. Why does preselling work so well? Because a sale via any affiliate program is really a two-step process. Your job, as an affiliate, is to presell customers and guide them to your merchant with an open-to-buy mindset. Let your merchant's site do its job and get the sale. I remember when I used to tell my star baseball pitcher, Joel Leonoff, "Joel . . . you don't have to strike 'em all out. You've got a great team behind you. Let them do their job." Same goes for your merchants. . . . Let them do their job. In other words, don't push your visitors to the click. Make them want to click. It makes all the difference if your visitors feel that it's their own idea. Here's a real concrete example. Earlier, I said that the key to success is to create a theme-based content site that is loaded with keyword-focused, content-rich pages. Now let's come up with a theme to show you how it's done. Your theme? Let's pull something crazy out of the air. Let's suppose you love concrete. Yes, cement! It's been your hobby, your passion, for years. Concrete statues. Concrete painting. Decorative concrete. Concrete in the garden. Repairing concrete. Various types of concrete. Hand trowels. Things to do with cement blocks. Concrete trade shows. Concrete and swimming pools. Concrete molds. Cleaning concrete. Ready-mixed concrete. Concrete countertops. Anyway, let's say that you decide to create a theme-based site that is all about concrete. Your home page explains how your site is the site for everything concrete—from structural to aesthetic.

You also, of course, create high-value, content-jammed, keywordfocused content pages. For example, your page about concrete statues

explains how to make striking statues for home and garden. You could even expand it into an entire statue section, with one page on the history of concrete statues, another one about how to market and sell the statues, and so on. The main point, though, is that you create truly excellent, highvalue content that delivers what your reader sought at the engines. You also weave relevant, in-context text links into the content as appropriate. Links to . . . • Books about the topic (e.g., concrete statues if that's what the page was about) • A garden supplier for concrete molds and trowels • Naturally, a concrete supplier! • Almost anything concrete-related See what's happening? By providing great content, you presell your reader, increasing your click-through traffic to your merchants and your conversion rate (sales). And by diversifying your affiliate programs among several related and excellent merchants, you develop multiple streams of income from one site. This is the way to go. Okay, we can summarize what we've learned in a key lesson to take home. I am giving it this title.

In other words, don't push your visitors to the click. Make them want to click. It makes all the difference if your visitors feel that it's their own idea. Here's a real concrete example. Earlier, I said that the key to success is to create a theme-based content site that is loaded with keyword-focused, content-rich pages. Now let's come up with a theme to show you how it's done. Your theme? Let's pull something crazy out of the air. Let's suppose you love concrete. Yes, cement! It's been your hobby, your passion, for years. Concrete statues. Concrete painting. Decorative concrete. Concrete in the garden. Repairing concrete. Various types of concrete. Hand trowels. Things to do with cement blocks. Concrete trade shows. Concrete and swimming pools. Concrete molds. Cleaning concrete. Ready-mixed concrete. Concrete countertops. Anyway, let's say that you decide to create a theme-based site that is all about concrete. Your home page explains how your site is the site for everything concrete—from structural to aesthetic.

CHAPTER TWELVE

Selling Information: Turn Your Ideas into Steady Streams of Cash Flow

From zero to $100,000 a year. Yeah, right! There are plenty of flashy Internet marketing gurus with their fancy e-books, training videos, and home study programs who claim they can show you how to make it big on the Internet. In doing the research for this book, I bought a bunch of information from many of them, and I learned something from every single one.

But do you know where I learned the most? By roaming around the Internet, finding stories of ordinary people who have come out of nowhere to create incredible streams of income. These mom-and-pop operators have found their niche on the Net and are pulling in the cash. If you love the free enterprise system, there is no story more inspiring than that of a person who's started from nothing and become successful. In this chapter, I share with you the stories of three such pioneers. Their product is information—their own information, packaged and sold over the Internet. At the end of this chapter, I share critical information about how to launch your own e-zine—an essential component of any successful Web site. How Perseverance Paid Off: The Ruth Townsend Story Ruth Townsend is a woman earning an income well north of six figures a year. Yet only a few short years ago, she was sitting behind the desk at a dead-end job. There are so many lessons to learn from this true story. I'll let Ruth tell it in her own words. Hi. My name is Ruth Townsend. No, I'm not going to tell you my age. It's a woman's prerogative to keep it a secret—even if those closest to me are always trying to pry it out of me! You won't find a photo of me, either. I've yet to have a picture taken that I like. Suffice it to say, I won't make the cover of the Sports Illustrated swimsuit issue, but I won't be the centerfold in Doggie's World, either. I live in the Finger Lakes region of upstate New York, where the summers are gorgeous and the winters brutal. Many times during the winter I don't leave my house for several days on end! Isn't it grand to work from home! I currently have a staff of one full-time and two part-time assistants, plus an office manager—Sara, my cat. As my business keeps growing, off-site office space may become a necessity in the near future. The office manager, however, has already put down her paw about not making the move! My background is in accounting and asphalt manufacturing and road construction. How's that for coming to the Internet and starting a thriving business from scratch? Just goes to show that you can be successful if you have a positive attitude, determination, commitment, and desire. Isn't that our choice? The choice to be successful? How did I go from a dead-end job to success on the Internet? On October 25, 1996, at 11:06 A.M., after 18 years of service to my company, I placed my keys and security card on my desk and simply walked out the door. I have not regretted it or looked back once. I was tired of the politics, the backstabbing, and feeling like a number instead of a player on the team. For me, it was the right choice and the right timing. (I don't recommend this for you unless you have a plan in place and finances to carry you for at least a year.) I had gotten to a point in my life where I had this feeling of emptiness. Have you ever sat quietly on a summer's eve or in front of a warm crackling fire and asked yourself, "Why am I here on God's earth. What is my purpose in life?" I've asked myself that question hundreds of times over the years and never came up with a satisfactory answer. A family, a home, a job, financial security, friends, and material things are all fine and dandy, but still I reflected, "Is this all there is? Is this all that there is going to be?" For several years I stewed over where I was and what my life was about. I wanted more. I wanted to accomplish something worthwhile. I wanted to sit up and be noticed. Maybe not in a big way, but I wanted to leave this world knowing that my life was more than just living, breathing, and taking up space on this earth. I had no idea how or when I would accomplish this, but I knew I was in a rut and my life was not fulfilling. I had goals and plans for where I wanted to be by the time I was ?? years old (thought you were going to get me, didn't you?). It just was not going to happen working for someone else. And it wasn't going to happen unless I did something about it. Then the Internet came along. It fascinated me. I still didn't know what it was that I wanted out of life, but I felt that the Internet had something to do with it. I just sensed that the Internet was the wave of the future. I didn't have a clue about what my business would be, but I jumped in with both feet and went for the gusto. And what a ride it has been! To get some money coming in the door, I started out trying to market one of those typical business opportunities. First I had to find some customers—so I launched my advertising campaign with the free classified ad sites. Needless to say, all that time I spent placing free ads only brought me other business offers. No one gave a hoot about what I had. The wind sure went out of my sails in a hurry. I think the only people reading the free ad sites are those who want to send you their own offers, which, of course, is not what you're looking for. When was the last time you browsed the ads at the free ad sites because you had nothing better to do? Then I heard the word e-zines. What in the world does e-zines mean? I soon found out that an e-zine is simply an electronic magazine—hence the word. E-zines are sent only to those people who have voluntarily requested them. Finally I had found a targeted market—unlike the free hit-or-miss ad sites.

Anyone can publish an e-zine. It can be about advertising, marketing, food/wines, multilevel marketing (MLM), parenting, sports, business opportunities, Web development—anything that a person wants to write about. Plus, some of these e-zines accept classified advertising. I started subscribing to some e-zines and learning about e-zine advertising and marketing methods. Ads displayed in these e-zines are seen by thousands of businesses and opportunity-minded people who voluntarily subscribe to these newsletters! I decided that this was the market I wanted to pursue—subscribers to e-zines. My first attempt at e-zine advertising brought 18 responses from four e-zines that had free advertising and a total circulation of a little over 3,600. I was in heaven! I finally got some responses from people wanting to know more about my business opportunity, not the other way around, which convinced me that e-zine advertising was the way to go! But I quickly found out I was faced with a new challenge, and again the wind went out of my sails and set my little boat adrift. With thousands of newsletters out there (I've seen estimates as high as 100,000!), how was I going to find only those that accepted classified ads? Working on a shoestring budget, I wanted to test my advertising with those e-zines that offered free or relatively inexpensive advertising. I started the routine of subscribing and unsubscribing to many e-zines in *an effort to discover those that accepted advertising. Once I started gathering and compiling data on the e-zines, it was easy to see that each had its own rules, regs, and how-tos of advertising with them. Little by little, I began to compile a storehouse of knowledge on each e-zine. There were so many variables! First I needed to know the subject material of the e-zine. No sense advertising a fishing lure in a food/wine newsletter! Then I needed to find out about the circulation. Paying $20.00 for a three-line ad or $20.00 for up to 10 lines was within my means, but it really didn't mean much without a look at the circulation numbers. If the circulation is 2,000 and the ad costs $20.00, that's $.01 per subscriber. However, if the circulation is 500 and the ad costs $20.00, I'm paying $.04 for each subscriber to see my ad. Publication and ad deadlines are important if you want to balance the amount of advertising that you have out each week. I didn't want one week of feast followed by one week of famine. Where do I place my ad? Should I send it by e-mail or place it online? Either way, I'd need the e-mail address or the URL. What are the payment options—pay online, send a check by mail, fax or e-mail my credit info? Maybe I don't want to give my credit card number online. Maybe I don't have a fax machine. Maybe the publisher accepts only checks by mail. It's important to know which e-zines will accept payment only by snail mail. You need to plan ahead.*

It's also nice to know if my ad is going to be posted online for added exposure. If so, maybe the cost of the ad isn't so bad! Well, you get the picture. Lots of time is spent researching all this information—reading each newsletter to find out how to place your ad. Maybe you need to send an e-mail to get more information. Then you wait for a reply. Maybe it will be a day or two before you get a response. Remember, you are not the only one asking for this information. I was getting confused and frustrated to say the least! So much wasted time each week trying to place my ads—with so few placed! I was looking for the missing pieces of the puzzle.

Remember, I was on a shoestring budget and every penny counted. I was looking for the biggest bang for my buck. I had to spend time researching the best deals. I couldn't place my ads in just any e-zine that happened to come along without knowing all the facts and being able to comparison shop! After spending considerable time with the search engines trying to find a resource that had all of the advertising information concerning e-zines in one place, I realized that no such resource existed. Then the lightbulb came on! I said to myself, "Why not create that resource yourself?" I put some feelers out to online acquaintances and found other people who, like myself, wanted to have all of the advertising information at their fingertips and in one place. E-zine publishers also saw the benefits of having a centralized listing resource. Their newsletters would no longer be lost in a sea of e-zines. Subscriptions would increase and advertisers would be pulling out their credit cards to place ads! I launched my business, Lifestyles Publishing, with the goal of being the Net's first directory of e-zines, complete with all of the information needed to place classified ads. It was scary to take on this project and to present it to the world, not knowing if I would fail or succeed. But I would never have known if I hadn't taken a chance on myself. This was what I had been searching for all of these years. Now the emptiness in my life has been filled with a sense of accomplishment and knowing that I am helping other people achieve their dreams and goals. The road has not always been easy, but I had a passion for what I was doing, and that is what it takes. Yes, there have been ups and downs, challenges of an ever changing technology, mistakes (but they are mistakes only if you don't learn from them), and trends that come and go. In a nutshell, that's who I am: someone who had a dream and the need to fill the emptiness in my life. I'm no super marketing guru here or someone who has the inside track to success—just someone like you who wants to succeed. I published the first resource tool that contains all of the pertinent advertising info needed to place ads in e-zines. As for the frosting on the cake,

I found my niche, and today I have a thriving, successful Internet business. Why am I telling you all this? First, countless people have asked me how in the world I ever came up with the idea. Now, you know. But, more important, I want you to know that you can find your niche, too. Take a look around you. Think about the problems, frustrations, or aggravations you may be faced with. Is there something you can do about it? Can you possibly come up with a solution? Can you turn that solution into a business that benefits not only yourself but others as well? It certainly can't hurt to take a close look at your situation. Who knows, you might be the next Internet success story! With passion, determination, and commitment, you can be, do, and have anything you want. Go get 'em!

CHAPTER THIRTEEN

EYEBALLS FOR SALE: MAKING ADVERTISING PAY

Kevin Nunley is an Internet marketing guru. Yet in 1996 he knew almost nothing about the Internet. He had been working for many years as a morning radio talk show host when he began to dabble on the Internet. Then, in 1997, his part-time, online activities hit critical mass. As he describes it, One day, 1 just got more business than I could handle, and it's been that way ever since. I left broadcasting to do this full-time. Every once in a while someone asks me why I'd leave the glamorous world of entertainment. I tell them that I now reach more people in a week—perhaps 1 million people— than I ever did in broadcasting. Articles I have written appear all over AOL, on dozens of major Web sites and e-zines—over 700 articles in all, floating freely around the Internet. Writing and publishing short, pithy, content-rich articles is Nunley's (he has a Ph.D. in communications, by the way) main way of promoting himself. He submits articles on marketing, advertising, and copywriting to various e-zines and content publishers. He receives no payment for his writing but e-zines include his byline and Web site address at the end of his articles—giving readers a chance to communicate with him. In fact, that is how

I learned about him. I was reading one of the many e-zines I receive weekly when I ran across Nunley's article about earning advertising revenues from your Web site. It impressed me, so I contacted him and asked permission to reprint his article in this chapter. Once again, another of his free articles will bear some fruit, as no doubt some of my readers will check out his Web site to ask about his services. In the course of building his business at www.drnunley.com, Nunley has acquired 6,000 subscribers to his own free weekly e-zine, DRNUNLEYS MARKETING TIPS. Because this chapter focuses on building advertising revenues at your site, let's go behind the scenes and see how Kevin Nunley generates advertising revenue from his operations. But first, I'd like you to read the article he wrote about Internet advertising. How to Sell Ads on Your Site Kevin Nunley Just about every Web site owner has thought of a day when they will be able to harvest huge profits simply by putting other people's ads on their site. Put up your site, insert ads, and wait for the checks to arrive. And why not? TV pulls down billions, your local daily newspaper probably gobbles up 80 percent of the ad money spent in your town, and your favorite top five rated radio station practically prints money. Media earns. So why can't your Web site get in on the media money frenzy, too? While Internet advertising has been a bit slow to get started (banner ad rates aren't any higher than they were in 1996), online advertising is starting to show signs of real promise. Optimistic predictions peg online ad sales topping $23.5 billion by 2005 That is even MORE than network TV earns. To make matters even more exciting for the small business owner, there don't seem to be many mammoth corporate sites running away with all the audience. Even Yahoo!, the king of Web traffic, is having problems keeping Wall Street happy. What to Expect Most Web site ads are in the form of banners. Banner rates are based on how many visitors your site gets. Just like advertising on TV or print, rates are CPM (cost per thousand visitors). The CPM rate for banners has been at $35 for years. I would be sloppy if I didn't also mention *that a great many sites discount their rates if you ask. In reality, the average CPM rate (when you ask) is well below $35. This sort of thing isn't at all unusual in the media world. I once worked for a radio station that had a published rate of $75 per commercial. Most clients got their spots for just $30. One major supermarket that had a knack for negotiation was getting the same commercials for just $ 12. One way to tell if a site isn't getting any advertisers is to note how many of their banners advertise their own site. Either they aren't getting anyone to buy their banner space or the rates are so low it is more profitable to advertise the company's own products. When you publish your ad rates, try to keep them high. It's much easier to negotiate a lower rate than to raise low rates later on. Most media profits come from higher rates. When your unique visitor count goes up, raise your rates. When an important writer regularly sends you content, raise your rates. Here's Who Can Place Ads on Your Site Fortunately, there are some very large and growing ad networks that bring thousands of everyday Web sites together. These well-organized packages of sites are very attractive to advertisers. Even for big companies, they are the way to go if you want to do an ad campaign on the Net without spending a month going from site to site setting up the deal. Make your first stop at TheAdStop.com. They include how-to advice and a host of reviewed ad networks that can get you started. eAds.com pays from a nickel to 20 cents per click and won't accept sites that get less than 100,000 impressions per month (an impression is when a visitor sees a banner). A site that is highly focused on a specific topic of interest to a certain valuable audience will produce better results for banners. eAds will negotiate a special price for sites with banners getting more than 500 clicks BurstMedia.com has taken the specialized site concept to a lofty level. They believe highly specialized site content provides better results for advertisers. On a recent visit, Burst was featuring LongHairLovers.com, a site for women with long hair. You may have noticed, as I have, that many women highly value their long hair. They regard that aspect* *of their person as very dear. You can imagine how personal the articles, products, and ideas featured at LongHairLovers.com can be to that specific audience. It turns out to be an outstanding place to advertise hair care products. Other ad networks go for hugely impressive numbers. ValueClick delivers ads to a global audience—including over 30 percent of Internet users in the United States. Banners range over 10,200 sites before 14 million people. In almost all cases, banners are served up on sites according to standard subject areas like Automotive, Business & Finance, Careers, and Consumer Technology. Mostly I've been referring to small business sites. If you are in charge of advertising for a larger corporation, you may need a more extensive and personalized campaign designed by an ad agency. Most top agencies, especially those hailing from New York City, have either established their own Internet ad departments or acquired smaller firms specializing in developing online ad campaigns. The big guys don't seem to have any special secrets. The current method is to search the Net for appropriate sites and negotiate a price. A recent report figured an ad agency worker placed dozens of calls and e-mails to get a campaign going. There are now efforts to build a database network that will speed up the process. How to Measure Your Site's Audience Most ad networks pay according to cost per click (CPC—how many people click on a banner) and cost per impression (how many people see a banner, usually sold on the classic CPM model I mentioned earlier). Before you get into the game, you need a good way to measure the number of visitors you get on each of your pages. Your numbers of unique visitors is most important. Your Web host may already have a hits measuring feature in place for your site. There are also software packages you can buy off the shelf and online services you can connect to. Perhaps the most popular and full featured is the free service at WebTrendsLive.com. The basic service requires you put their button on every page of your site. You can pay more to go buttonless. You get real-time traffic analysis and a gaggle of reports on visitors, page views, ad campaigns, and revenues.*

When you can view your audience from every which way, you can bet there is at least one perspective that makes your site look extremely attractive to advertisers. Maybe you don't get a whole ton of visitors, but those who come spend an hour clicking through every page on your site. That shows visitors value your content and don't mind giving up a considerable helping of their valuable time. That is a quality that would mean sales for many advertisers. In the end, you may find it's the MEASURING and not the ads that make you the most money. Keeping a constant eye on your site's stats lets you make better decisions on where you place content, what kinds of content you use, what products and services you sell, and how you run your own ad campaigns. This invariably helps your site make more money from the sale of products, services, subscription fees, and through more efficient spending.

If you stand back and view Nunley's marketing efforts, you can see that it forms one great cycle. He writes articles to publish in e-zines. This effort gleans customers for his own e-zine. Then he narrowcasts his own e-zine to his 6,000+ subscribers, which generates paying customers for the services he offers on his own Web site. As gravy, he gets the spin-off advertising revenue from selling ad space in his own e-zine. At this time, he does not sell banner ads on his site, but that may be only a few clicks away, as the traffic to his site increases and the number of his e-zine subscribers mushrooms. This is a perfect model for you to follow. Here is my advice to you: "Go thou and do likewise." To round out this chapter on earning advertising revenues from your site, here's a great story about someone who made a killing by creating a Web site specifically designed to generate advertising revenues. The story is submitted by Corey Rudl, one of the Internet's leading marketing gurus. You can visit Corey at his famous Web site at http ://www. marketingtips.com/freebook. I strongly encourage you to sign up for his free newsletter. It's full of fabulous information. Take it away, Corey. There are two basic approaches to making money from your Web site. The first is what I call a portal Web site, and the second I refer to as a sales Web site. A portal Web site is specifically designed to generate the bulk of its profits from the sale of advertising. A sales Web site is designed to generate most of its profits from the sale of products and services. If you have a portal Web site, your goal is to get as many visitors to your site as possible by enticing them with something special that you offer. You might provide them with valuable information, help, free software, entertainment, or something similar. There are countless possibilities! If you are giving away something of value, you will attract traffic. Hotmail offered free e-mail accounts, Yahoo! gave away search information, financial portals give you instantaneous financial news, and so on.) Offer something unavailable anywhere else and give it away free—that's how to generate traffic. You may be asking, "How do I make money if I give it all away for free?" Once you are established and attracting high-volume traffic, you can make money by selling advertising space on your site or by offering products or services. This is a great way to profit from traffic, even if you have nothing to sell. The traffic itself becomes your asset! This is particularly true when the traffic that you are generating has very specific interests or needs. Advertisers are willing to pay good money when their ads are being directed at large numbers of their target market. Let me give you an example of how developing your own portal Web site could be your key to success in online marketing. Although the general details are true, the names are fictitious. I think you'll agree that it's an amazing story! A friend of mine (let's call him "Michael") had a new-car-invoice dealer-cost-pricing business. What's that? Well, say you want to know the price that a local car dealership *paid the manufacturer for a certain vehicle. You just go to his site, pay Michael $15, and he'll send you an e-mail with a breakdown of exactly what that dealer paid for that car. Sound like a great service? It is! With this kind of knowledge, you can go back and haggle with the dealer for a really good price and probably save yourself hundreds (maybe even thousands) of dollars (all because you know what the dealer paid for that car). Pretty powerful! Is it worth $15? Absolutely.*

Michael was selling this service like hotcakes. People were coming to him and buying three and four reports at a time (one for a Subaru, one for a Honda, one for a Toyota). He was making $100,000 a year doing this, and it was taking him only one or two hours a day. Pretty easy income. I have a second friend we'll call "Chris," who came to me one day and said, "You know what? I can do better than that! I'm going to give it all away for free!" He rented (for $2,000 a month) the actual database that provides these car dealer cost invoices. Then guess what he did? He started giving away for free the same information for which Michael had been charging $15. Chris set it up so that you can go to his Web site, punch in any car you want, any year you want, and you get the price. How much does it cost you? Nothing—not a dime! Next, Chris approached all of the big car sites saying, "Why link to places that make you pay for car-pricing information? They charge $15 and I'm giving it away for free! Link to me!" The logic proved irresistible: They all started linking to him. These links generated hundreds of thousands of visitors to Chris's site every month! Big sites like Road & Track and Motor Trend began funneling traffic into his site because he offers such a great service. Instead of linking to Michael, they link to Chris. Now they can say to their customers, "Look! We're great because we're telling all of our clients where they can get this great free *information!" They even published editorials about his site in their magazines. After six months, Michael just couldn't compete. His income dropped from $100,000 a year to barely $15,000, and he lost his business. However, Chris wasn't making any money, either! He still had to find a way earn a living. The database was costing him $2,000 a month in rental fees, and basic necessities such as rent and food cost another $1,500, for total monthly expenses of about $3,500. Chris had only about six months' worth of cash in the bank! Now what? Imagine what a powerful site this could be! The traffic Chris generates is very specific: people in the market to buy a vehicle. Even better, after six months his site was generating high-volume traffic—300,000 people every month! Guess what Chris did? He called companies like Toyota and Honda and said, "Hey guys, would you like to advertise on my site? I'll only charge you $35,000 a month each." Honda said, "We pay $30,000 a month to put a one-page ad in Car and Driver. You're going to let 300,000 people that have a direct interest in buying a car see our ad? That's a great deal! Of course we'll advertise with you!" Talk about a target market! And $35,000 is a bargain! In his first month Chris made over $100,000 in revenue. Why? Because he was willing to lose money in the beginning to offer a valuable service (the portal model) so he could make the money on the back end. Chris created a portal Web site: He drove traffic to his site and then converted it to a profit model after six months. But Chris wasn't done yet! He called me up and said, "Hey Corey! Can I sell your book, Car Secrets Revealed, at my site?" I said, "Sure. I'll give 10 bucks for every one you sell." Now he sells my car book at his site, and every month I send him a check for thousands of dollars in sales! Even better, he started selling extended warranties and insurance quotes at his site, generating even more income for himself through referral fees. It was incredible! Within a few months, Chris was approached by someone who said, "I'll give you $1 million for 20 percent of your business, and I'll kick in all the venture capital you need to develop it." Wow! What do you think Chris's answer was?*

How long did it take him to build a successful company? Less than a year! He now has a million dollars cash in the bank plus millions of dollars in venture capital that he can use for whatever he wants! Today Chris is running a big office with lots of employees and programmers . . . the whole nine yards! The beauty of this is that he started with nothing but an idea. An incredible example showing the potential of Internet marketing. Portal sites do not generate instant cash. They require a good six-month investment (and sometimes years depending on your idea) of time and money. However, once these sites are successful, they pay off big, and the time commitment and maintenance from that point on is minimal. To sum up, the risk is big, but if it works, the payoff is big. Most people are unwilling to risk six months of their lives only to find out that the portal does not work and it was all for nothing. . . . Conversely, a killer idea can make you a fortune

CHAPTER FOURTEEN

NAKING MONEY FROM THE INFRASTRUCTURE OF THE NET

You've heard it said that the only people who made money in the California gold rush were the people who sold picks and shovels to the miners. While you're laying claims to your Internet fortune, you can always keep money coming in the door by supplying the necessary tools for the millions of Internet miners. What kinds of tools do they need? The Technology to Host and Run a Web Site Business Internet service provider (ISP) Web hosting Web design Autoresponders Listserves Shopping carts Credit card services Daily troubleshooting Web site statistics Product Services Product design Manufacturing Printing Warehousing Inventory control Shipping Marketing and Advertising Services Advertising Copywriting Marketing strategy Joint ventures During the early days of the Net, a lot of money could be made in Web site hosting and site design—because only the geekiest of geeks had the technical expertise to do the work. Now, with free, automated, templated Web design solutions (see, for example, Bigstep.com in Chapter 9), even everyday technophobes can build their own Web sites. These technical services will become increasingly commoditized. Translation? Too much

price competition will cut profit margins to the bone. Don't try to compete in this arena. Neither will there be easy pickings in product services. The real opportunity is in the area of marketing services. By becoming a marketing expert for hire, you will have a steady supply of new clients while gaining experience to expand your own Internet business. Now more than ever, the fundamental principles of marketing are desperately needed by millions of newly launched Internet businesses. In other words, I'm going to encourage you to learn the principles of marketing, to become one of the best—a pro. It is the most important business subject you will ever learn. The best products in the world gather dust in the warehouse without good marketing. Even successful offline businesses need help marketing their products in the confusing new field of the Internet. Since most of these businesses will be desperate for immediate solutions, your services will be in high demand and deeply appreciated. There follows some excellent marketing advice for offline businesses. The advice sounds almost too simplistic. Yet I'll wager that there is not one business in ten in your city today that is practicing this obvious business strategy to boost sales. This lesson is provided by Corey Rudl, an Internet marketing guru who, as a young man in his late twenties, makes over $5 million a year dishing out practical tips for building business (see www.marketingtips.com/freebook).

How to Make Money with Your Offline Business by Using Online Technology! I would like to take a moment to speak with those of you who are operating an offline business. Have you stopped to consider how the Internet could improve—even skyrocket—your business profits? Most people do not realize how important it is to give their offline business an online presence. They do not believe that online marketing would work for their particular business. Guess what? They're wrong! Online marketing can be applied to every business . . . no matter what kind of product or service you sell! You don't believe me? Let me give you some examples. . . . Let's say you own a hair salon. Obviously, people are not going to search online for a hair salon—they're going to look in the Yellow Pages or get a recommendation from a friend. Your hair salon caters to a local market, not a global market. So why should your salon be online? If you're a smart entrepreneur, every time patrons come to your salon to have their hair cut or colored, ask for their e-mail address while they are paying. Put it into a simple customer database at your cash counter and make a note of the date and the kind of service that you performed for them. There is a lot of power in doing something like this! Why? Because three weeks later when you realize that business is slow, you can simply sit down and send your customers an e-mail. Dear [insert customer name here]: Thank you for your visit on February 10 for the cut and perm. I just wanted to write and thank you for your business. I also wanted to let you know that for the week of March 3, 2000, we're offering a special 20 percent discount on haircuts to ail our valued customers. However, you must book your appointment within the next 48 hours to get this discount. Just call us at (310) 555-1212 right after you read this and we will book an appointment right away. We look forward to seeing you again soon! Sincerely, Your friend at Chop & Frizz Hair Studio I will explain a little later how you can address this e-mail to all of your customers (whether 100 or 1,000) individually (e.g., "Dear Tracy") and send them all out by pressing one button. If you have collected 500 e-mail addresses in the last two months, it will take you about five minutes to write the e-mail and about two minutes to send it to all your customers. Once you've sent out your e-mail, your phones will start ringing and the seats of your salon will fill very quickly. Will this technique generate more business? Definitely! How much time did it take you? Almost none! Did it cost you anything? No! Let me give you another example. . . . How could a grocery store profit more by using online technologies? Once again, you can use the Internet to keep in touch with your *customers and improve your customer service! Simply get the e-mail addresses of all customers who walk through the cashier line and let them know that you'll be sending them discount coupons every week. By doing this you are going to remind thousands of people, "Come back to our grocery store because we're going to give you 30 cents off yogurt and a dollar off milk." Are they going to come back? You bet! All you need to do is remind them that you're there. And it costs you nothing! It's all free with e-mail! Which grocery store do you think they are going to visit? I won't even bother answering that. . . . You know which one! Do you know how much it costs stores to produce newspaper flyers touting their specials? Tens of thousands of dollars a week! Guess what? If you e-mail those specials to your customers . . . it is now free . . . and you get to put tens of thousands of dollars directly into your pocket because you don't have those high advertising costs anymore! This is the beauty of the Internet. Every business—I don't care who you are or what you do—should be online. If you're not online and using the technology to increase your business, you're losing money Is this going to make you rich? No, it isn't. But you will surely earn more money than you are making now in your business (sometimes 50 percent more). Think about it, and use the Internet creatively. Don't just do things the standard way. Be unique! Use online technology to create the kind of rapport and loyalty that turns a first-time customer into a lifetime customer! What do you have to lose? If you e-mail your customers and only a few respond with only minor additional sales, who cares! You can't fail. Any incremental sales that cost you nothing add to your income. It is "free money," as it cost you only about eight minutes to prepare an e-mail and send it to all your customers. With technology today, it's so easy to do! For about $100 you can pick up a small database that is fully mail-mergeable. You can use this database to enter your customers' names, their e-mail addresses, the most recent day they were in, the purchases they made, and the services that were performed. Later, you can use this information to send out thank-you notes,* *surveys, and promotion or contest information—all of which will help you build a relationship with your customers and create the loyal clientele base that every business needs! Even better, with the software that is available today, you can fully automate these tasks. After taking five minutes to write your thank-you notes or promotional letter, you can simply click a button and, voila, your letter has been sent out to hundreds or even thousands of customers. One excellent piece of software that will do all this for you is Mailloop. Mailloop is great because it acts as a customer database, a bulk e-mail server, a newsletter server, a Web form processor, and an autoresponder. All the software you need is included in a single application! I personally use this software and highly recommend it! I couldn't imagine doing business on the Internet without it. For more information on what it does and how it works go to http://www.marketingtips.com/mailloop. By providing this kind of amazing service, you're going to make your customers feel special. Your business will stand out in their minds because you have taken the time to develop a bond—a feeling of community— that draws them back. It's easy to do, it works, and it takes no time at all when you use the right software. However, I need to warn you that this is not going to last forever. Get in while the getting is good! Soon, more entrepreneurs like yourself are going to smarten up and realize that these kinds of techniques could really improve their business. But guess who will have beaten them to the punch? You! Because you knew about it first. Get in there! Get your offline business online. You will see nothing but benefits. Increase your business by developing a relationship with your customers! It takes almost no time and costs practically nothing. . . . How can you lose? The only*

CHAPTER FIFTEEN

Treasure Hunting: Turning Junk into Cash with Auctions

Let's start with an article in the Wall Street Journal. It will blow your mind. Yard Sales in Cyberspace— Want Barbie & Ken Salt Shakers? Goat Pictures? Just Click and Bid by George Anders After months of trying to run a variety store in this coal-mining town, Wayne and Shanna Bumbaca realized that their shop wasn't going to make it. They put up a "Closed" sign and carted home the vestiges of Rocky Mountain Discounts, including their most foolish purchase: 144 red Santas with tiny helicopter blades attached to their heads. The Christmas ornaments lingered in the young couple's garage for weeks. "We couldn't give them away," Mr. Bumbaca recalls. "I put them in my yard one day with a sign saying Tree,' and no one took them." Then Mr. Bumbaca tried listing a helicopter Santa for auction on the Internet. His initial asking price: $2.95. Late that evening he got electronic mail from a woman at a U.S. military base in Italy, offering $8. By the way, she asked, were any extras available? "I woke up my wife," Mr. Bumbaca recalls. "I said: 'Honey, I think we're on to something.' " That was in May 1997. Today, the Bumbacas are selling 800 items a week online, putting them on pace for $600,000 of revenue

this year, much of it windfall profits from customers who can't resist making sky-high bids to win an auction. Other people leave the house to work. The Bumbacas simply pile inventory in their garage and then spend most days at a personal computer in their living room, running a giant yard sale in cyberspace. As Americans become spellbound by the Internet, thousands of ordinary people are recasting themselves as online merchants. It's easy to see why. The Internet's reach is so vast—and its ability to connect buyers and sellers is so quick—that anyone with a modem and a cluttered garage can dream of becoming a high-powered sales machine. Some 2.1 million people use the biggest online auction company, eBay Inc., and thousands more are rushing to join a similar service just launched this week by Amazon.com Inc. In cyberspace, even the weirdest listings find buyers. Pictures of goats sell. Life-size cardboard cutouts of Xena the Princess Warrior sell. Salt-andpepper shakers molded to look like Barbie and Ken sell. "At first we worried a lot about what to carry," Mr. Bumbaca says. "Then we realized it didn't matter. We've got two million people looking at our listings. There's always someone who says: That's exactly what I want.' " Whether this boom will last much longer is an open question. Selling online is no refuge from bad checks, angry customers or aggressive competition. And as the number of merchants explodes, there is a growing likelihood that the novelties and outright junk for sale will far exceed anyone's demand. What's more, many small-time Internet vendors are acutely dependent on steady shipments of cheap merchandise from major manufacturers and distributors. It's no great challenge to open up these suppliers' cartons and then sell items, one at a time, on the Internet at a hefty markup. Distributors might wake up to the juicy profits being made and use the Internet to sell direct to the public themselves. If so, cyberspace could become rough territory overnight for many mom-and-pop merchants. In the small towns where grass-roots Internet marketing is most alluring, however, no one wants to brood about such problems. "Selling online lets me compete with

Wal-Mart and Sears," says Mike Baker, a Springdale, Ark.,

dealer in posters and celebrity photos. Just a year ago, he was a shift supervisor at a Levi Strauss & Co. factory, about to lose his job in a plant closing. Now he works from home, selling more than 10,000 items a year online. Fueling this trend is eBay, which each day lists more than 1.8 million items for sale, ranging from antique clocks to car stereos. Users provide all the listings, stock the goods themselves and negotiate prices among one another. EBay simply runs the Web service and collects a token listing fee, plus a commission of 1.25% to 5% any time a sale is completed. The genius of this arrangement is that users' own activity generates organic growth—letting eBay expand rapidly without having to do much of anything. "A lot of people think we're this quaint, inconsequential trading service where people just buy a Furby or two for Christmas," says Steve Westly, eBay's vice president, marketing. Not so, he declares. He calls eBay the Amway Corp. or Avon Products Inc. of the 21st century: a wide-ranging sales network that draws its energy from an elite group of top sellers who live and breathe their company's way of doing things. Last autumn, eBay singled out 10,000 people—the top 0.4% of its registered participants—and dubbed them PowerSellers. They get personalized Christmas cards from the company. An in-house newsletter celebrates their accomplishments. Not everyone is thriving. But many retirees, stay-at-home moms and disaffected office workers are making thousands of dollars a month on eBay, letting blue-collar America taste a little bit of Internet riches. In Wyoming, the Bumbacas typify this new form of commerce. A bumpy dirt road leads to their house, where three preschool children watch cartoon shows most mornings or race outside to play on a swing set. There's no storefront sign, no corporate stationery and no dress code. From the moment they wake, though, the Bumbacas are dead serious about their enterprise. Mrs. Bumbaca, 27 years old, is the purchasing and marketing expert. Almost every day, she flips through distributors' catalogs, looking for nifty items to sell. Victorian art prints are current favorites, especially pictures of elegant ladies and jolly children. But when a visitor tries to peek at the front cover of a catalog, she quickly pulls it away. "We can't tell you the names of our distributors," she says. "That's precious information." Once the Bumbacas decide what to carry, Mrs. Bumbaca writes short, joyful descriptions of each item, to be posted on eBay. A Victorian lamp is "beautiful." A koala bear print is "adorable." Such headlines catch people's attention, she says. Then serious shoppers can click the listing to see a digital photo, scanned in by her husband. Each week, the Bumbacas list about 2,000 items on eBay. Auctions typically last a week, letting people around the globe compete to be high bidder. Only about 40% of the goods sell on the first try, but duds usually can be remarketed at lower prices. When a listing catches fire, the Bumbacas can watch as prices soar, minute by minute.

At times, Mr. Bumbaca winces at how much people will pay. Cardboard cutouts of John Wayne that cost him $14, for example, often attract dozens of bids and sell for more than $40. Economists call this "the winner's curse," and they say eBay is a prime example of the way that competing bidders will work themselves into an irrational frenzy for something they think is scarce. But if customers really want something, the Bumbacas say, it isn't their role to limit the price. Each evening, after their children go to bed, the Bumbacas dash off 100 or more e-mails to winning bidders, telling them to send payment to Sheridan, while advising that goods won't be shipped until the checks arrive. "I try to be as friendly as I can in two seconds," Mrs. Bumbaca says, "but I don't have the time to do much more." Mr. Bumbaca is the lucky one who collects the morning mail, jammed with payments from dozens of faraway places. "It's like going fishing!" he says, giggling, on a recent morning as he tugs an enormous clump of letters from his mailbox. Recently the Bumbacas hired two *full-time assistants to help process the barrage of orders. Because eBay's brand of commerce links total strangers, there is always the risk of a transaction going sour. The Bumbacas say that, to their surprise, they have been stuck with only about a dozen bad checks, while handling 40,000 shipments. But they have been briefly misled by pranksters, including a Massachusetts boy who placed a $10,000 order for 100 cowshaped clocks, with no intention of paying. Meanwhile, a handful of customers have complained that the Bumbacas can be annoyingly slow in shipping merchandise. "We've got our share of growing pains with this business," Mr. Bumbaca concedes. A bout of flu knocked out his family in February, and it took weeks to get caught up. The basement shipping department, run by Mr. Bumbaca, is an exercise in anarchy. Every corner is jammed with art prints, clocks, posters and shipping cartons. A tractor is nearly invisible in the garage, buried under hundreds of mailing boxes and tubes. "It used to be even worse," Mr. Bumbaca says. "We lived in a smaller house until a year ago, and we had filled up the baby's room with boxes. There was just a tiny path that let us get to his crib." Most small businesses lease a postage meter for $30 a month or so. Not the Bumbacas. They hold down expenses by buying stamps once a week. But as their shipping volume soars, their postage needs are overwhelming Sheridan's post office. Each Monday, Mr. Bumbaca buys about $1,300 of stamps. Twice this year, he has emptied out the local inventory of highdenomination stamps. When he asks a clerk: "Do you have an armed guard to walk me to my car?" no one is quite sure if he's joking. For eBay's most intense PowerSellers, the online auction company can be the most real thing in their life. The Bumbacas hardly know their neighbors.*

But they swap Christmas presents and family updates with favorite customers in Hawaii and Michigan. Mrs. Bumbaca pores over her feedback rating on eBay every day, cherishing 3,000 positive comments from various customers and *wondering what she did wrong to deserve 53 rebukes. And when the Bumbacas' three-year-old daughter, Mallary, was learning to talk, one of her first words was "eBay." Some day, Mr. Bumbaca says, it won't be nearly so easy to make a good living from an Internet flea market. He got an ominous warning of changing times when a fishing-lure distributor withdrew exclusive rights to sell on eBay. The Bumbacas dropped that product line rather than fight it out with unwelcome new competitors. "We weren't doing that well with it anyway," Mrs. Bumbaca says. But if their top distributors tried something similar, that could hurt business more severely. For now, the Bumbacas are thriving—to the point that they are becoming local legends. A few weeks ago, a man in Rapid City, S.D., called Mr. Bumbaca to ask for advice about selling Indian handicrafts over the Internet. "I told him: 'This sounds like a consulting situation,' " Mr. Bumbaca recalls. " 'My rates are $40 an hour, if you want to come out here and talk.' " "I didn't think we'd ever see him," Mr. Bumbaca says. "But the next Saturday, he drove 225 miles to see us. We ended up talking for four hours—and he paid us right away."**

When you read a story like that of the Bumbacas, doesn't it make you believe that you, too, could pull off something like that? The next story I'm going to share with you is not quite as dramatic, but it's a great success story in the making. Our ordinary-people success story regarding auctions is about Robbin Tungett. You can find her at www.auctionriches.com. Her eBay ID is robbin. Up until three years ago, Robbin was the office manager for an industrial supplies company (valves, plumbing supplies, etc.), where she had worked for eight years. She started to dabble in the auction field on eBay and caught the bug. She would work nine hours during the day at her regular job and then come home and spend another nine hours figuring out the auction game. She immediately began to make money, expecting every month that the money would end, but her *income from auctions soon exceeded her salary. Within 18 months she quit her job to pursue auctions full-time. My first real auction success was a product I created to help people set up their auction businesses. It was called Handy Home Page Helper. It took me two days to put it together—a neat little product, mostly information and links to some free software that people can use to format a nice little auction ad with colors. My husband laughed when I told him what I was planning on doing, but when I sold 194 copies at $10 apiece he stopped laughing. I've probably sold over 20,000 of them in the past three years. On my Web site, I sell it for $14.99. On my auctions, it usually goes for about $9 or $10. My cost is less than a dollar. I must admit, the auction business has gotten quite a bit more commercial in the past year, so the prices aren't as good as they used to be. But there is still plenty of profit for the person who is willing to stick it out for the long term. This type of home-based business gives me the freedom to choose whatever hours I want to work. I work best at night, so around midnight I begin work on Web site design for other clients (which is another one of my income streams) and go until about 4 or 5 in the morning. Then I go to bed. I get up around 11 A.M., check my e-mail, and fill a few orders. I spend most of the time answering e-mails. I'm a one-person business. Recently, I needed to come up with some extra cash quickly, so I created another product to auction. It's a CD-ROM called Auction Riches. It contains five different items (wholesale sources for various products, how to make money with your Web site, accepting checks online, etc.). It took me a day and a half to put it together. I burned in my own CD and immediately put it online. It's selling very well. After a while, you learn the tricks of this business. I noticed that most people didn't have any pictures on their auction site, so I added my picture and sales increased right away. People don't want to deal with a nameless, faceless entity. If they can see you're a real person, it's easier for them to trust you.*

I try to keep my prices under $10. I think it's better to sell cheap because if people feel they got a good deal they might check out my Web site and buy from me again. In fact, that's one of the major advantages of having an auction site—it gives you the opportunity to advertise your Web site. Every Web site that sells anything online should have an auction going on. It gives you great exposure. Online auctions offer an excellent opportunity to make money online! There is no other opportunity that allows everyone the ability to play on a level playing ground, whether you're just looking to make a few extra bucks a week to pay the babysitter or hoping to earn a full-time income! Whether you are a work-at-home mom making a modest income or a big company with lots of inventory to sell. . . everyone has the same opportunity to reach literally millions of people! Think about it. With only a little computer knowledge and a good auction ad you can be selling things at a profit in your first week! Selling on online auctions can be very profitable! Not only that, but it can actually be a lot of fun as well! There is nothing more apt to put a huge grin on your face than going to your mailbox and finding it stuffed with envelopes full of money! Literally tens of thousands of people are making a full-time income with their online auction businesses! I've asked Robbin to share some more of her "multiple streams of auction income" wisdom with you in the next few pages. She has graciously agreed to share some of the tips that have taken her several years to learn. What Are Online Auctions? Online auctions have been around since the mid-1990s, although it wasn't really until the late 1990s that their popularity began to explode. EBay.com is the king of online auctions, and while they are still the most popular, there are now literally thousands of auction sites to choose from. Many, like eBay, are general, person-to-person auction sites with many categories covering just about anything you can think of.

New, specialized auction sites pop up every day. Online auctions provide a forum for anyone to sell just about anything. Most auctions charge a small fee to list your item for sale, plus a small commission once the item is sold. When you list an item for sale, you choose the opening price. From that point, those who are interested bid on your item. Most auctions run for a predetermined number of days. At the end of that time, whoever entered the highest bid wins the item. When you place an item for auction, you are promising that you have the item available. When you bid on an item that is up for auction, you are promising to pay the amount of your bid plus any applicable shipping and handling charges if you submit the highest bid. It works much like a live auction except for the fact that the bids don't continue for as long as people are bidding. Once the auction is over, it's over. When you win an auction, you remit the money to the sellers. After the sellers receive your money, they send you the item you bid for and won. It takes a lot of trust to send money to a stranger. Of course, mail order has been around for a long time, and many of us have sent money to brickand-mortar companies trusting that we will receive what we paid for. With online auctions, though, most often you aren't dealing with companies—you are dealing with individuals who may or may not be honest. This is where feedback comes in. Feedback is essentially the online auction user's reputation. It is a type of rating system that allows bidders and sellers to leave comments about each other. It is the only way for other bidders and sellers to find out who is trustworthy. Normally, there are three kinds of feedback: positive, neutral, and negative. Obviously, if you have a good experience dealing with someone you would post a positive comment. If you've had a really bad experience that couldn't be resolved you would post a negative comment. Neutral feedbacks do not express strong feelings one way or the other. Each positive comment results in a gain of 1 point, each negative one results in a loss of 1 point. Neutral comments neither add nor subtract from the rating. While viewing people's feedback files can help ease your mind about doing business with them, people who are just starting out have no feedback or perhaps a very low feedback rating. In this case, you have to make a judgment call and trust your instincts. Everyone starts at zero. Just because a person doesn't have a high feedback rating doesn't mean that individual isn't honest.

www.ingramcontent.com/pod-product-compliance
Ingram Content Group UK Ltd.
Pitfield, Milton Keynes, MK11 3LW, UK
UKHW021911190726
13853UKWH00002B/625